A Jacana book

D1330658

Child Soldier

Fighting for My Life

China Keitetsi

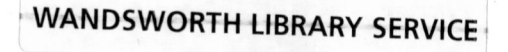

First published in 2002 by **Jacana**
5 St Peter Rd
Bellevue
2198
www.jacana.co.za
e-mail: marketing@jacana.co.za

© 2002 **China Keitetsi**

ISBN: 1-919931-19-8

Cover design by **Disturbance**
2nd floor Innesdale
101 Innes Road
Morningside
Durban
e-mail: disturb@mweb.co.za

Edited by **Ruth Friedland**

Page design by **Lynda Harvey**

Printed by **Formeset Printers**
22 Kinghall Ave
Eppindust
Cape Town
7460

This book is printed on environmentally-friendly paper.

Dedication

I would like to dedicate this book to all child soldiers who are still alive, and to those who didn't make it. May your souls rest in peace.

I would also like to take this opportunity to say goodbye to my son's father, the late Lieutenant-Colonel Moses Drago Kaima.

Acknowledgements

My gratitude goes to the Danish people and their government, my new family, the Hansens, the United Nations staff in South Africa, N Omutoni, Richard, Robert, Emanuel, Lucky Dube, Thor Kujahn Ehlers, Jens Runge Poulsen and his family, Melissa Stetson, my teacher Søren Jesperson, Birgitte Knudsen, Eskil Brown, Søren Louv, Pia Gruhn, Dennis Hansen, Kenneth Hansen, Lisa and Kenneth, my doctor Lill Moll Nielsen, Lars Koberg and my late mother.

My thanks go to Major General Fred Rwigyema, Uncle Caravel, my sisters Helen, Margie and Grace, Lieutenant-Colonel Bruce, Lieutenant-Colonel Benon Tumukunde, Major Moses Kanabi, Major Bunyenyezi, Captain Kayitare, Afande Ndugute, Corporal Kabawo, Private Sharp and all those brave soldiers in the NRA who decided to give their lives for the sake of Uganda.

It is so hard to accept that you are all gone. I know I have to stay strong and try to prevent this terrible tragedy from happening again.

Foreword

I AM CHINA KEITETSI, former child soldier from Uganda. I was resettled in Denmark by the United Nations in 1999. My story is about my life as a child soldier in Yoweri K Museveni's NRA, now the UPDF.

This book all began when Birgitte Knudsen, head of the Integration Office of my Danish commune, suggested I write down all my pain. My tears ran with no end. The more I wrote, the more relieved I felt. When I had written more than a hundred and fifty pages, I told Knud Held Hansen, my new-found father what I was doing. He said, "Oh! You are writing a book!" The book has helped me come to terms with my new life and made me see that it was not only my soul that needs help – so many others are still there. Writing down my experiences helped me to single out the abused from the abuser. Now people write to me from around the world through mail, e-mail or by signing my guest book on my website. Everyone seems very touched by my story and ready to do something to make a difference. My story reaches all people, regardless of their rank in society.

So far I have met UN Secretary General Kofi Annan, Olara Otunnu of Children in Armed Conflicts, Nelson Mandela, Bill Clinton, Whoopi Goldberg, Harrison Ford, Robert De Niro, even Graça Machel and Queen Sylvia of Sweden. Meeting Nelson Mandela was unforgettable. My head dropped onto his chest and my tears began to flow. I can't find more words to describe how I felt at that moment, but I felt the answer with my heart. Mandela said, "I have written a poem for you" (it is called "For Ishmael and I"). "Now you have to listen as I read it to you," he said. I watched him as he read words of love and peace, and my tears just fell.

I hope that the African edition of my book will make people aware of the terrible suffering of child soldiers on this continent. To make that difference is my purpose in life now – I don't want to hear or see any child going through the same long road I went through.. My eyes look up in the sky and all I see are the moving clouds and not my friends. My childhood is long forgotten. Sometimes I feel as if am 6 years old, and sometimes it's as though I am 100 years old because of all I have seen.

Contents

Part One Who is My Family?

Part Two Into the Fire

Part Three A New Family

Part Four Survival

Part Five A Way Out

Epilogue

A Word to Yoweri Museveni

Part One

Who is my family?

Madness at Home

MY FATHER WAS BORN and studied in Rwampala, a small village in western Uganda. His first job was as a manager at the coffee marketing board. Later, after having met my mother, he decided to study law.

When I was born everything changed because I wasn't a boy. In 1975, my father divorced my mother and she left our home when I was six months old. Looking at the world with the eyes of a young child, I couldn't know what the future held for me. My mother was forced out of her home and forbidden to ever return, and if ever she tried, her life would end. In Uganda the most powerful thing between a man and woman, their love, decided her fate. In their relationship my father had all the power and would not share it. My mother had no other choice but to leave me, though she knew very well that I would never get a chance to grow up like most other children.

I was too young to understand my loss and do not remember much from those times. Today I sometimes sense a feeling of extreme loss, so different from my other emotions, and a flood of sadness and power-lessness flushes away my last thoughts. When I am back in reality, and I try to track through my life of memories and emotions, I always get into the swamps of forgetfulness probably caused by the loss of my mother.

I could not understand that I was a poor child who had been left with a father who was more like an animal, like a predator, than a human being. I was a nuisance to him, having to be taken care of every minute of the day, so my father got rid of me by sending me to the farm where his mother lived.

My grandmother was not pretty like other old women I had seen. She was large and short, with one eye that cried all the time. Her mouth faced to the east and whenever she opened it to talk it seemed to struggle to escape by flying away, but her old muscles always held it with a firm grip. I was less concerned with the way she looked, as long as no-one made me kiss her.

I had learned now that my father owned lots of land with banana-plantations and all the farm animals you can think of, but the animals I loved most were the goats. The farmhouse consisted of five rooms, built with clay-bricks and covered by a tin roof. At the end of the house, in the fifth room, was what I considered my grandmother's biggest asset, the banana-storage. And through her window you could see a grass field full of pumpkins, that in my eyes seemed to just be there by coincidence. I don't remember the taste because we never tasted them.

I guess I had a huge play-ground, and I remember that in my first years of life I was made a bit "savage" by those surroundings, something that I never really got rid of. During those days another old woman, my father's aunt Florida, came to live with us, and when I compared her face with my grandmother's I found her charming and beautiful. I wished to be a boy and grow older.

My grandmother was always shouting at Florida, and I was confused, not knowing why my grandmother was so aggressive. Whenever my grandmother started swearing at her, she would only stare back and showed no sign of trying to defend herself. That made me dislike my grandmother and I was convinced that Florida could have far more power if only she would defend herself. I knew that I had to make it my responsibility if I wanted the two to fight with their fists, and soon I was busy searching for the perfect way to start a fight.

One fine morning I woke up, and nobody was at home. I went to the corner in the living room where the milk was stored and filled a pot until it became heavy. Then I went to my grandmother's room and as I was pouring the milk on her bed sheets, I thought of how she would react if she caught me, and I quickly ran to hide in the bush.

After some time I asked myself: "Why am I hiding, when no one has seen me?

"This is stupid," I said aloud, and left the hiding place. But when I was almost home, I remembered that they would ask who had been drinking the milk. "Should I go back to the bush? No, go home," I said to myself, and on my way, I passed the goats and calves and stood staring at them for a while. I then went home and sat in the garden, and waited for Florida and my grandmother to return. After a time I heard grandmother ask me about the missing milk, and with my red sleepy eyes I told her the goat had asked for it and that I had given it to her.

"Which one of them?" She asked with her big voice. "The white and black," I replied with my little one. "We have many that have those colours," she said. "Jaah, the one with four kids." She burst into a rusty laugh and if I had not covered my ears, I would have lived without them until today. When she laughed, I said to myself, "Grandmother, laugh now because you will cry later." I was sure Florida would beat her. They began preparing supper while I sat beside them like a dog waiting for a piece of meat. Yes, my eyes might have been looking at the meat but my mind was on my grandmother's mouth, thinking of how it would look after the fight. Maybe then it would face to the west for a change.

In the evening, grandmother was outside in the kitchen, calling my name. When I got there she told me to help her hold the lamp because the moon, which normally lit the open kitchen, was not clear that evening. Our kitchen was an ancient design, without chairs and with a fireplace made of three stones above the fire for the cooking pot. My grandmother was sitting down on a little piece of cloth while I sat on the dusty ground, giving her light from the fuelled lamp. When the oil was ready she began cutting the onions, and now her other eye too dropped tears. I felt like laughing, but I got angry at the same time, thinking that her tears might fall in our food. Accidentally one of the tomatoes fell down, and I was told to point the lamp where it had fallen. I saw the tomato between her legs, and when I was about to pick it up, I saw something that looked like a small animal with black fur. "Au!" I shouted.

"What is it?" she asked.

"It's an animal with black hair!" I replied.

"What are you waiting for? Burn it!" she commanded, and in a flash I grabbed a big fire stick and burned it. She jumped up, screaming in a high-pitched voice. But I continued trying to have another go because I wanted the animal, which was stuck, to leave. After she had slapped my cheek I stopped, but she told me to leave the kitchen anyway. After supper I sat in a corner like a shadow and stared at them, until grandmother ordered me to bed. Reluctantly I left, but I felt disappointed because I had wanted her to go to bed first, so I could enjoy the war between them.

As I lay in my bed, I began to question my actions. I found them mean and ugly, but still I didn't think I was wrong. A few moments later I heard my grandmother moving towards her bed, and I became frightened, so I covered my head with the blanket and waited for her to turn into a screaming monster. I waited for some time, but still nothing happened. It was already morning when I woke up. I jumped out of bed fearing that I might have missed the fight, which I had arranged and hurried to see if they had fought in silence.

When I finally reached the living room, I couldn't decide whether I was disappointed or relieved. I discovered that nothing had happened. Even when I looked at them carefully I could not see any scars. I kept wondering but I could not figure out what had stopped grandmother from raising her anger, "Maybe I didn't use enough milk," I thought.

The next day, my grandmother went to the banana plantation leaving me with Florida. She was sitting down in the little garden beside the house, where I then went and sat down very close to her. "If I tell you a secret, will you keep it to yourself?" I asked. She smiled beautifully, but her eyes were blinking as if she was about to cry.

I began telling Florida about my feelings towards my grandmother. I also told her what I had done the day before. She moved closer, I suppose, to hear more, but I was already busy with something else, sneaking with my eyes to see whether she also had "the black furred animal". "Don't look there – stop it!" she said. Then she warned me about my grandmother, telling me I should never do such a thing again. I could not understand why her eyes were wet – I expected her to be happy about what I was trying to do for her. After talking to me she put me to bed.

A few months later, Florida fell sick and spent most of her time in bed. I was sad all the time, seeing my grandmother shouting at her whenever she asked for something to eat or drink. One evening I went and sat beside Florida's bedside waiting for her to hold my hand as she used too, but her hand remained by her side. I took her hand and shook it, but she remained still. I went outside and told my grandmother but she ignored me and washed the dishes. I started crying, thinking my tears might move her. Instead she shouted at me to keep quiet.

My grandmother went to Florida so I decided to stay away. The next thing I remember was my father in a white car in front of several other cars. Inside the house I saw my father cry, while everyone inside was quiet. Then people went to see Florida in her room. When they came out they were grey and sad, or quieter than before. I became angry when no one could tell me what they were crying for – then my grandmother began to cry too. At first I was shocked, but then after a second thought I had a closer look – it could as well be spit that she had put there below her eyes because I couldn't imagine her crying for real.

After many tears Florida woke up and suddenly the whole place was different. People who had been crying were now happy, all laughing and drinking and singing. My confusion was total and I thought that my father and the rest had turned mad.

Then my father ordered the workers to slaughter some goats. I stood near them and looked at the blood as it flowed away. I loved those goats – they were like my children. I even had names for them. I cried and ran inside, leaving the madness for Florida.

I woke up the following day and found Florida in the living room, still looking sick. I sat beside her and asked if she had heard people crying. She told me that she must have been in a deep sleep and heard nothing. But when I looked at her eyes I saw tears. Then she told me that she was leaving with my father to go to the town house, and she felt sad leaving me behind.

I begged her to stay but she told me that she would only be away for a few days. A few days was a long time and I could not convince my broken heart. So I ran away to the stables of the goats and calves. I sang to them while my tears ran onto the goat I embraced. After a while I got angry. I couldn't accept what Florida had told me, and now was the time to stop my father from taking her away from me. I ran home as fast as I could but found that she was already gone. I turned to look at my grandmother and thought about Florida, asking myself if I would ever see her again. Tears clouded my eyes and I cried many times over the loss of Florida, but they never brought her back to me.

The Lion and his Mother

AFTER FLORIDA LEFT, things got tough for me. All the love had gone and it felt as if my heart lost some of its life, making the days long and grey. My grandmother started turning everything around on me. She stopped changing my bed sheets, and one day she told me that I had to learn how to wash them myself. "Stop peeing on them!" she had shouted, making it sound as though I did it on purpose, to annoy her.

That night I tried to stay awake – the only solution I could find to my new problem She had told me I would be punished if she ever found a wet bed again. When I slept everything was quiet and warm, and I dreamed of peeing on the toilet. It felt good as my pee left me in a slow motion.

I sat on the wet bed for some time, trying to find how to escape punishment. I went outside and poured some water in a cup. I poured the water on the already wet bed sheets and screamed for help. My grandmother's old legs came running to my bedside and she asked me what had happened. With the cup in my hands I told her that I drank some water, and then the cup slipped right out of my hand. She looked me in the eyes for about five minutes without blinking and said, "Tell me the truth," in a low voice. I felt a strange cold creep upwards from my tailbone to the back of my neck. With a dizzy head and pounding heart I told her I had peed on the bed and I was afraid of her.

Even before I could shut my mouth she grabbed my arm with her strong old hands and dragged me outside. I had nothing on. In the surrounding bush she plucked a stinging nettle with her other hand and beat my whole body with its burning leaves. She left me there screaming and crying as I tumbled around with my skin on fire. I cried half the day, and refused to put on my clothes, thinking that I was punishing her. But I soon realised that I only punished myself. I could not understand why my grandmother treated me like this, and her punishments just kept on getting worse.

One evening my grandmother came to wake me up and saw that my dress was wet. She grabbed my arm like an angry lion and threw me to the floor. I heard a sharp snap followed by a strong pain tearing me apart from my elbow to my neck. Still I struggled to get up, but when I looked at my arm I stayed down. A white bone had penetrated my skin but by far the worst shock was my own blood. Seeing it brought back the memory of the goats being slaughtered. I saw their blood and their life faded away. I cried and screamed, and my heart was beating so fast that I thought this would be my final day. My grandmother shouted at me to keep quiet, and then set my bone in its right place. The pain came back as hard as before. However, I feared my grandmother more than my pain so I remained quiet. When she had finished, she took me to bed again, and without a word she left me alone to cry in silence.

It must have been a Thursday when she broke my arm – she knew that my father would be there on the Saturday. I remember – he always came with the sunset, to check on his livestock and pay the workers. On that morning my grandmother ordered me to lie, to tell my father that I had fallen. She warned me that if I didn't, she would beat me again after my father went back to town.

She left me at home and went to the field for a few hours. When we finished eating, I went to sit where the goat kids were playing and jumping but I was sad when I remembered the good times I had had with Florida. After a while I stood up and walked to the road, sat myself down with my arm on my lap, and began singing in silence.

Suddenly I heard the sound of a car. I stood up and listened intently, hoping to see my father. A blue Suzuki car was driving towards me. I waited to see who it could be. A beautiful, tall woman got out, and my eyes caught up with her smile. Her teeth were white as snow, and when she smiled the second time, I hoped she would keep on smiling.

When she came nearer, I noticed a white bundle in her arms. A man stepped out and it was my father. I stood there smiling, waiting for him to hold me only he was too busy exchanging jokes with the woman. I was puzzled by the way my father looked at her, it seemed as if he was about to bite her. When we were about to go into the house I took off my long sleeved T-shirt and showed him my arm, and before he could ask me anything I told him the lie. He held my arm looking at it with intense eyes, before he asked who had tied on the sticks. "Grandmother," I replied.

"You'll be alright" he said, and went inside. I followed from behind and went to a corner of the living room where I remained standing, hoping to catch his attention. No one seemed to notice me, so I decided to go outside.

Before I got to the door the woman called and asked if I wanted to hold the baby. "Where is the baby?" I asked. They smiled and she told me to come and see. Sitting down the way she told me to, she put a child on my lap, while she kept her hand supporting its head. I was about to ask her whether it was a boy or a girl when it threw up on me. I told her to take her baby. She did so, telling me that it was a boy. Then I asked her who she was, and she said she was my mother.

I went back to my goat kids with renewed hope.

New Mother

FINALLY IT SEEMED AS THOUGH there was someone to free me from my grandmother. My new mother asked me if I was happy about her coming to live with us, and there was no doubt in my voice when I replied, "Yes!" I had a good time with my mother, but I became more excited when my father and the workers began building a new house for my mother and I. The new house was about two kilometres away from grandmother's house, and it had more rooms.

The cows and the goats were moved from grandmother's house to our new place. My mother seemed to control everything, apart from one banana plantation, which remained in my grandmother's care. My father returned to the town house, leaving my mother and I at our new home. I trusted her and told her everything about my grandmother. She seemed to take my side and I was overjoyed. I thought that I was pleasing her, and like any other child, I was jealous of my position of trying to find favour in her eyes. I exaggerated and even lied to her when I told her about things my grandmother had not done. I don't know how and where she gave birth to her second child, a girl called Pamela.

I was pleased because I had another child to be with. One day my mother left me at home with Pamela and I was puzzled when she said I must not let Pamela cry. At first I had a good time with my baby step-sister, until I tried to make her sleep. It didn't take long before she woke up and began to cry. I tried to feed her. I tried everything, but she just kept on crying until her mother returned. Before I could say a word she grabbed Pamela and blamed me for not having fed her. Though I was very hurt by her accusation, she scared me too. I saw her face twisted with anger, so I remained silent.

After feeding her baby, she put Pamela to sleep and my mother came back for me. I was shocked and unable to defend myself. She turned into a biting dog, pulling my lips and ears and pushing me down. I lay on the ground quietly, trying to understand, but when I tasted my blood on my lips, it didn't matter. The seed of hate for my little sister was sown. I was certain that if she hadn't cried it wouldn't have happened.

Every time I looked at Pamela I felt like pulling her ears and lips like her mother had done to me. My sister became my enemy and whenever she cried, my heart would beat with fear and hate because I knew my mother would punish me. The love I thought would last forever between my mother and I was fading.

Some time passed and my father returned from the town house. During supper, my mother told him I was wetting the bed every night, and she was getting tired of changing the sheets every morning. I watched her telling my father these lies and it hurt me that she was trying to put a knife in my back. I was the one who made my own bed! My mother was a liar. But the look on my father's face made me keep quiet about it.

After supper, my father told me to sleep on the sofa. He said that if I wet it he would beat me the following morning. I went to bed with fear and promised myself that I would not fall asleep. The first thing I did when I woke up was to check the sofa. It was wet. "No!" I cried in a whisper, covering my head with my arms. I went to sit in the early morning sunlight as I waited for my father to wake up and do what he had promised. After my father beat me, he told me that I was not allowed anything to eat until supper time.

I saw the love she showed to my younger sister and brother and I was envious. Then an old woman called Jane came to our farm, and they told me she was my grandmother on my stepmother's side. I was nervous, wondering if she would live with us and add to my misery, but she left a few days later.

A month or two later Jane returned with all her belongings, two daughters, a son and a few cows. Not only was I forced to call her two girls "aunt", but I also had to call her son "uncle", although he was almost the same age as me. Everything about them annoyed me. They were wild, eating each and every thing that came their way, and I wondered if it was the first time they had seen food. Every day I hoped they would go back to wherever they came from and leave our food alone.

Around three days after the new family had arrived, my father returned to show them where to settle. I was torn between the two families because both grandmothers required my services. I was sent with parcels of food and other appliances to each house, and soon there were so many parcels that the two old women began questioning me about what the other had. Jane was a lazy old woman, who preferred me to stay and do a little extra work while her children played. When I got back my mother would beat me for being late. No one ever said thank you. I felt that everybody was spinning around me giving orders, and I urgently needed to stop it as my strength and sanity began to fail.

We had many different kinds of poison but I had no idea of how they worked. Once in a while the cows needed to be cleaned because of parasites. It was a demanding job, requiring all the family to go out and spray disinfectant liquid on the cows. And that's when I thought of a possible escape from my torment.

I pretended to be sick so I could stay home and try some of the poison. When everyone had left I took a stick with milky poison on the end and pointed it at the cat. After the cat had finished licking it, it started to spin around and then ran outside. I followed, realising with fear and sadness what I had done as I looked at the cat's newborn kittens playing and tumbling after me. I went into the bush and began searching for the cat, crying tears of regret. I could not find her. I stood still for a while, focusing on everything that caught my eye. I sat down on the grass in the sun and dried my eyes. I remembered the cat's life and what good times we had had together.

I remembered the black fur around her yellow-green eyes and her fat, strong body. She only ever drank milk so we were sure she remembered her job and that she would never wander far from our house because of the armies of rats camped there. She was always welcome indoors and she spent a lot of time there with her kittens. Often when someone got home she would look at the person and pretend she didn't notice. When you sat down, her eyes would open wide. If she was not already near you, she would try to approach in a nonchalant manner, a little eager to get the act right. Then she would wait a while before jumping into your lap and making herself comfortable.

I became frightened. "If I give my stepmother and Jane the poison would they spin around and disappear as the cat did? Would they come back?"

My mother and Jane returned. They found me where I was sitting after my search for the cat. I was very hot from the sun and my sadness made me look ill. Later they heard the kittens' cries, and wondered what had happened to the cat. I told them I didn't know, as I had been asleep. However, I still felt guilty. I wanted to tell everyone what I had done, and every day I hoped the cat would return.

Dangerous Mind

WE HAD TWO SMALL LAKES – the furthest one was the only one the cattle could drink from. The other one was very close and easy to get to. The problem was its water was dirty. It was torture going to that lake without shoes because of all the trees and their thorns. One evening I returned with the calves, happily singing to them. I stopped when I saw my stepmother standing with folded arms in front of the little calves' shed. "Why did you take them to the bad lake, do you want us to lose them?" She began questioning me. I tried to defend myself by denying her accusation even though she was right.

She started walking towards me with a stick in her hand, so I took a few steps back. "Do you want to kill them all?" She shouted at me with an angry voice. I told her I loved the calves and I would not do anything to harm them, only her madness got worse and I had to tell the truth.

"You are not afraid of eating but you are afraid of hurting your feet. I'm sick and tired of feeding you. It would be better to feed a pig!"

How could she say this? She arrived without anything, only her son with a cloth wrapped around him. How then could she think this way as if she owned the food that I had. I thought she didn't know what she was talking about, but of course I kept my mouth shut. I knew I wasn't going to eat for another day or two, so I turned my face away like a hungry dog, hoping she might feel sorry for me and forget what I had done.

"Go to bed! No supper for you, and don't think I've finished with you," she shouted. Slowly I walked away like an unwanted dog with its tail between its legs hoping once more that she would have some compassion and tell me to come and eat. But she never did.

That night I couldn't sleep – my stomach was crying out for food. At about two in the morning I got up. I was surrounded by darkness so I kept my eyes closed as I slowly moved towards the door to where the

23

leftovers were kept. I got hold of a pot, and started to gobble down the food as I listened for any sounds that might cause me trouble. I got back into bed with a smile, as I thought that now I would be able to sleep.

Early in the morning I hurried back to the pot and smoothed away the marks of my fingers, but then I noticed the sides of the pot still showed that somebody had eaten out of it. I realised that my worries about that pot would never end, and I decided to wait outside for my lesson.

My mother came and said to me, "From now on you will be doing each and every thing that has to be done". Then she went back inside, leaving me wondering whether she was going to find out about the missing food. I stood there waiting for her to return and when she didn't, I went inside to check if she had gone through the back door to her mother's. But she heard me from her bedroom and told me to cook some milk. I was hungry, but I was afraid to ask for breakfast. When I had finished cooking the milk I took a cup and began pouring the hot milk. I had to hurry in case I was caught and I forgot the heaviness of the pot. I missed the cup and poured the milk on my leg. The pot fell to the ground and I started to scream. She looked at me and said, "Your big stomach will bury you one day." She went back to the house complaining about the spilled milk.

I went to a tree, picked some leaves and covered my burn with them but they wouldn't stay on, and I began to cry. I tore off a piece of my clothing and tied it around my leg. Then I sat down against a tree and watched the calves play.

It didn't seem to matter what I had done to myself, my mother always insisted I was able to work.

Three days later she told me to go and check on the calves down in the field. Before I got there, the cloth fell off my burn. I picked it up and thought I would check the wound later. When I reached the calves I sat down slowly and untied my wound and discovered little white things. At first I thought they were strings of the cloth that I had used to bind my wound, but when I tried to remove them I discovered they weren't cloth but maggots! I screamed and ran home as fast as I could, crying and thinking my leg was rotten. My mother helped me to remove them and covered my wound with cottonwool. It didn't help me to get rid of the fear that I might lose my leg, so I checked it each minute of the day.

The next day I had to bring some milk to my grandmother. She was not home when I got there, so I sat down in the garden and waited, thinking about my pain back home. I felt sad and didn't want to return. Then I saw a machete lying in the garden. I took it in my hands and looked at it. I saw flashes of blood in front of me. I put my thumb against a piece of wood, closed my eyes and chopped it in the middle. When I opened my eyes, a piece of flesh was hanging from my finger with blood beginning to cover my feet. I tried to cry to ease my pain but my eyes remained dry. I was in pain but happy at the same time, being sure that now my grandmother would let me stay with her. Leaning against the wall, I watched my finger bleed. My wish to stay was so strong that I even squeezed the wound when the blood showed signs of stopping.

Soon one of the workers, Byoma whose name meant "metal", came to fetch me. Byoma was a funny looking man, with muscles all over and hanging lips that made him look like a cow waking up. When I told him that I could not walk, Byoma only shook his head and went back from where he came.

When my grandmother finally came past and asked me what had happened, I told her that a man passing by had taken the machete from the garden and chopped my finger. She asked me if I knew the man. "No," I replied as I noticed the wrinkles on her face increase. She panicked before getting a basin of water to wash my finger, and I just managed to hide a happy smile as she bandaged it. As soon as she had finished she looked at me and said, "Now you can go home." I walked through the grass and woods feeling sad, thinking of the machete, my finger, the blood and pain – all for nothing.

When I got home my father had returned from the town-house, but he had gone to check on the cows. In the evening he returned and I went to greet him, trying to look as if I was dying. "Take off the cloth," he demanded, and gently I took it off. I noticed a change in his face, a look of pity, which made me feel secure and I came closer to his lap where I laid my arm. He turned my hand around before asking me what had happened, and with tears in my eyes. "Grandmother did it!" I said, and I managed to squeeze out another tear. He looked down for a moment, still holding my hand. Then he stood up all confused and began walking around the house. Soon Byoma walked in and before he could say a word, my father told him to go and call Grandmother. My tears dried fast as I realised in fear that he had decided to ask Grandmother about it.

I thought of telling him the truth. I went outside to where he was standing with the calves, but his shouting scared me back to the sofa where I remained seated until my grandmother arrived. She sat down beside me, and as she was about to greet him, my father started shouting at her that she was nothing but an evil old woman who only thought of herself. Grandmother didn't have any idea of what was going on, so she asked him to calm down and explain. "Go away from my house," my father told her before he went outside. She turned to look at me and asked whether I had any idea of what might have made my father so upset. My answer was to shake my head. I didn't wait for more questions so I ran to my bedroom leaving her alone in the living room. I heard her talking with herself before she left and I was satisfied with my revenge on her for not letting me stay at her home. I had to stay in my bedroom to control my excitement.

Now that I had injuries I could no longer watch over the goats and calves though I still had to take over my mother's sister's duties, bringing food and other supplies to their mother every night. There were no roads from my father's house to Jane's, just a path with wild grass and other plants. I felt very afraid of being out there among the wild animals, and she always sent me in the evening after the cows had been milked and the food had been cooked.

Weeks went by without any problems until one day I heard what sounded like the screams and shouts of drunken people. Shocked, I stopped and listened intently, but heard nothing more. Convincing myself it was just my imagination, I went on.

The next day I heard a hyena howl and it made me very afraid. It was dark, making it impossible to know if they were near me or not. I stopped for a long time, arguing with myself about whether I should go back or go on. I had to choose between being caught by the hyenas or by my mother waiting at home. I chose to wait for the hyenas to come and get me, but they never did, so I went on. When I reached the house I told Jane I had heard hyenas, hoping that she might let her daughters escort me back home. To my disappointment she did not seem to care. I went back to the darkness of the road by myself, singing in a loud voice to ease my fear. When I reached home I pretended nothing had happened because I knew Jane wouldn't care anyway.

One day I heard the hyenas howling very close to me, so I ran back home, thinking they were about to attack me. When my mother saw me return without giving Jane the food she demanded an explanation. I said, "But I heard the hyena howling near me, and I thought that they were too close and that's why I had to run away."

She told me for the second time that I knew nothing but to eat and that I shouldn't return before having delivered the food.

I looked down, feeling the whole world was against me, and returned to the loneliness of the night. I wished that I were a bird flying high above the dangerous animals, feeling helpless because I knew I couldn't be a bird, and there was nothing else to do. All I could do was cry at the side of the road. I looked around and saw the bush covered in darkness and heard only the sounds of night birds.

I started walking again. Suddenly I felt pain go through my heel. I ignored it and kept on walking. When I reached Jane's house, pain covered my whole leg. Jane knew immediately that it was a snakebite and fear gripped my heart because I knew that snakes were dangerous. At once she examined my heel, cut it with a razor and put medicine in the wound. Then she put something on it that appeared to be sucking the blood out of my veins. I was especially afraid when nobody would tell me where it was taking my blood.

But it was heaven not having to walk in the darkness. I got a crazy idea of beating my leg with a wooden stick every time it showed signs of getting better because I preferred the pain rather than being sent back into the darkness. I never condemned the snake, only the one who had sent me to it!

The Bees

ONE DAY, MY MOTHER WENT to the town house and I had to stay with my grandmother and babysit my sister, Pamela. My grandmother used to go to the banana plantation every morning but with the baby and me there she had to take us along. Grandmother was marching in front with Pamela on her back and a hoe on her shoulders. I had a five-litre container full of water.

When we reached the banana plantation I looked up at the sun and realised it was eleven o'clock. Grandmother left Pamela and I under a mango tree, while she went behind a banana plant to change clothes. I left Pamela and I tried to sneak up on Grandmother to see how she looked without clothes, but again the little thing prevented me from having fun, as she began to cry and I had to run back and hold her mouth. When Pamela had stopped trying to bite my hand we looked up and saw Grandmother moving away from us to begin planting the beans.

Soon I left Pamela playing and went to the other trees filled with oranges. When I looked up at the trees I got a nice surprise. I saw a huge beehive. I could not wait as I imagined the sweet honey dripping onto my tongue.

I noticed a long stick lying there, as if it was waiting for me, but before grabbing it I remembered my grandmother who fortunately was happily buried in her own glories. I took the stick in my hands and looked at it for some time before I jumped over to the tree and began to swing the stick at the beehive. My low height and thin arms almost failed me, but it was a shame for me just to give up and I fought with the hive until it landed on top of my head, breaking into many pieces and releasing thousands of furious bees that covered my head. With one arm I swept away the bees from my face as I tumbled over to Pamela and grabbed her with the other, and the bees followed, stinging both of us. I tried to run away with Pamela but no matter where I ran the bees followed from behind. She started to scream so I put my hand over her mouth and nose so Grandmother wouldn't hear what was happening.

I was stung all over as I couldn't protect myself with my own hands, and I kept my own mouth tightly closed because it seemed that was where the bees wanted to go. When running didn't help, I tried rolling on the ground with Pamela, but still it didn't work so I screamed for my grandmother's help. We were already stung badly, but at that moment I only saw the terror of what would happen to me when my grandmother, stepmother and my father saw us. Grandmother heard the screams and came to our rescue. She grabbed one of my arms still holding tight around Pamela and we ran away. When we reached the other side she took Pamela away from me, looked at her and screamed. After she had gained her breath back she took me by my left hand and led us home, shouting at me all the way as if trying to drown the noise of Pamela's desperate cries.

When we reached home she placed Pamela on the sofa and began writing a quick letter to my mother and father before she gave it to one of the workers who then hurried to the town house. After she had finished everything, she ran back to Pamela, grabbed her and began picking the stings off her body. All that I could see from the distance was my grandmother's hand picking and throwing away, and I knew the old woman's eyesight so I was never sure whether she was picking the right things. I could do nothing but sit, trying to be as unnoticeable as I possibly could. My situation was getting worse, but Grandmother seemed blinded by Pamela's swellings. I had never felt so much pain before. When I finally tried to get some help from her, she just turned away from Pamela for half a second and gave me a look from the eyes of a beast. Her eyes made me think of how they would torture me when they got back, and the thought made me so scared and angry that I started cursing myself.

I felt like an outcast. My grandmother reminded me of the punishment I would get, so I went outside and sat on a stone nearby the house. My eyes were closing because of the swelling. I went to my bedroom and tried to sleep but my fear would not let me. Just as I was about to fall asleep, I heard my mother scream and I knew she had seen her daughter. Then I heard my father's footsteps coming closer and his voice commanding me to come out. I became so afraid that I hid beneath my blanket and wished everything would go away. But he just threw away the blanket, grabbed me by my neck and dragged me to the living room. He sat down in front of me, and demanded to know what I was doing with the trees. "I wanted honey," I said. He replied with a heavy clap on my fat cheek, saying, "Honey, honey, honey…" Then he went away. I stayed there waiting for him to return with a stick. After beating me, he called the doctor. I heard the doctor ask him why it looked as if I was beaten, and my father told him that I had fallen while running away from the bees. I listened to my father's lies and wished that I could stitch his mouth closed.

My Beautiful Kids

SOME TIME AFTER MY FATHER LEFT, my mother punished me by making me look after the goats without realising how happy this would make me. I was away from morning till evening, away from the beatings and insults. I was pretty happy at my new job, the goats obeyed me and gave me no trouble, and I enjoyed seeing my mother watching me every morning as I walked to the bush pretending to be in misery.

One day with my goats I discovered small white mushrooms, which grow during the rainy season. They are considered to be a delicacy.

The only thing that made my job a little difficult at times was that the goats didn't talk, and I needed someone to talk to or joke with.

I left the goats alone for a while and went to our neighbours, though I knew very well that they were my father's enemies and I felt good inviting them to my father's field. The mother was sitting outside talking to two other women.

When I showed them the place where the mushrooms were, I went back to get my goats. Then I sat myself down in the grass with my bunch of bananas and watched them walking around the mushroom-field. That night I went to my bed with one wish. I wished that I would find more and more mushrooms. In the morning my mother gave me a cup of milk and told me to finish up quickly and take the goats to the field, and then she went outside. When I could no longer hear her footsteps, I went to the kitchen, grabbed a peace of meat from a pot and stuffed it into my mouth. The meat got stuck in my throat and when I struggled to spit it out I got tears in my eyes. Just before I lost all my breath I ran and grabbed a cup of water. I sat down and breathed heavily with relief. After I had gained my senses back, I went outside and took my goats to the field, telling them about my horrible start to the day.

We arrived at a nice spot with grass where I left them eating and went to search for mushrooms. When I had walked for some time without luck I heard the sound of a goat's kids, not far from where I was standing. I responded by mimicking their little voices and four beautiful kids tumbled towards me from the thick bush. I felt like crying, but when I realised that they all were little girls like me, I stopped crying and I found myself laughing. The little kids followed me and joined the others, and I was thrilled with my new discovery, thinking that I finally had found something that would be mine. All that filled my thoughts was that now I had my own little family and I would never be sad again.

After I had finished my duties for the day I couldn't wait to give my family the good news. I thought they would be happy for me, having found these little friends, and I expected them to give me encouraging words. I arrived home smiling and proud. But they didn't even smile and my grandmother only said, "We will see them tomorrow." When I saw their faces empty of any emotion, my happiness vanished and I was confused and sad. No one said anything the next morning. I could only wonder… would the goats be theirs or mine? I did not understand. A few weeks later my father came home, and I forgot all about greeting him as I took his hand and dragged him over to the goats.

"You've got yourself some beautiful goats," he said. "You have to take good care of them because they are still very small." I told him I would take good care of them because I loved them, and he left me full of happiness with the confidence that now they belonged to me. But I was proved wrong later. Perhaps I misunderstood.

As time passed my goats delivered and I found myself with twelve kids. It was a holiday, and the whole family gathered at the farm. The day had come for me to be baptised. I woke up early in the morning, and while getting dressed I heard my father through the window telling Byoma to slaughter two goats. I watched my goats being pulled by my father, pulling them with a rope to get them under the tree where the workers slaughtered animals.

I knew I had no power to stop him and I began to cry. Byoma began tying their legs. My grandmother grabbed my hand and we headed to the church where my mother and father in Christ were waiting. These people were appointed to be like my godparents to me. We waited for Father Robert to arrive, and I felt devastated by the sweet music that only increased my sadness. As Father Robert approached the altar I saw everyone stand up. The next thing I noticed was my new name being called. After a gentle push from my grandmother I reluctantly went up to the altar. As I came back my mother in Christ gave me a hug, asking me why I was sad.

I sneaked out and left the rest to finish the ceremony. I didn't want to ever go home again. Instead I went to the banana plantation to my hiding place, with a bunch of bananas. I was thankful for not going back because I knew that if I had done so I would have had to eat my friends. I wanted to punish my father and Byoma by drinking the poisonous milk so that I too would spin around and disappear as the cat did, but I was too scared. Instead I thought what might happen if I disappeared.

I stopped at a big tree, trying to find a lie to save me from a beating. But I couldn't find one so I decided to walk into the house with an angry face. My father, mother and my grandmother were in the living room. They all turned and looked at me. My father stood up and shook his head, and then walked towards me. With a firm grip he began pulling my ears, telling me they had been looking for me everywhere. Soon we were outside.

While my father beat me I saw my grandmother and my mother looking from the window. I held back the tears so they would think I wasn't in much pain, but what I didn't realise was that my silence made my father beat me harder. When he finished I ran behind the house to the garden where I let the tears go.

I woke up later on and it was pitch black. At first I didn't know where I was until I realised how cold I was in the night air. I listened carefully through the night birds singing, but I could hear nothing else in the lonely darkness, apart from the frogs and the hyenas. I became frightened, but it felt even worse to go and knock on the door. I decided to sleep with the goats. The smell didn't matter at all, I was more worried that the goats would trample me but when I got in they were calmly sleeping.

The next morning, I discovered that my dress had blood on it and one of my fingers was broken. I sat in a corner, folded my arms against the early morning cold, and waited for my family to get up. I listened very carefully to my pain, but found only anger. I cried again, wishing I had a shoulder to cry on. Instead I found only the wind and wished to be free the way it seemed to be.

My father came outside, and when I looked at his face I wished a big stone would drop on his head. I saw the guilt in his eyes when he looked at me, before lowering his head like a thief. "Father, my finger is broken," I said. Without a word, he walked down to the same tree where my goats were slaughtered and looked up at the sky, and after a while he walked back, passed me and went inside.

He returned with a knife and a piece of wood and sat on a stone, cutting the wood into small pieces. I wondered what the wooden pieces were for. I hoped not to be roasted on them. After he had finished, he took me inside and washed my injured hand, but when he began tying the sticks around the broken finger, I felt pain but didn't want to show him. I coughed instead and as he moved, bad smelling air escaped him. "Can he also fart?" I was surprised because I had never heard any sound like that before from the older ones. "You're full of my goats, maybe that's why you fart," I thought with sadness growing inside me. I promised to revenge my friends when I grew up and this feeling only grew stronger as I was forced to eat my friends later, one by one.

I was getting desperate. I couldn't sleep. All the voices of my goats sang in my memory. To revenge this I thought of feeding my fathers' cows poison, but after I imagined the mess that the cows would leave behind after spinning around, I changed my mind.

Far-Off Dreams

I WAS SITTING UNDER A tree enjoying the cool freshness of the wind. When I looked down the road I saw a young boy coming towards me. I had a strange feeling as he looked at me with very gentle eyes. He made me feel completely safe in his presence and I hardly noticed when he was close enough to touch me. He asked me how I was. I told him I was fine and kept looking straight into his eyes. He asked me whether my father was in. I nearly said I had no such person, but I did not know the man so I kept it to myself. I told him to wait and that I would call my father.

But as I started walking the man shouted at me to come back. He asked my name and asked me whether my grandmother lived with us. "Yes, she is here at the moment, but she has her own house," I replied. His expression changed. I sensed an eagerness when he asked me politely if I could call my father. My father said, "Tell him to come here." The boy came with me as I had asked, and when we reached the doorsteps my father was resting against the door with lowered eyes. He seemed to recognise the man. He told the man not to enter the house, to wait outside. The way my father welcomed the man made me want to hear more, so I went to a hiding place not far from them. I heard my father ask the man what he wanted in his home, and the boy began to weep, telling him he had nowhere else to go.

"You know I told you never to come near my home! What do you want from me?"

"You are the only brother I have," he replied. When I heard the word brother I knew this man was my uncle, and I listened intently without missing a word. My father gave my uncle a few minutes to act on his threat. Then my uncle answered. "Where do you want me to go? Please help me!"

I could feel my uncle's helplessness, feeling helpless myself. What amazed me most was the look on my mother and grandmother's faces.

My father kept getting colder towards my uncle who, at the end, knelt down and begged him. I started to cry silently. A few minutes later I saw my uncle leave. I had to know the truth so I hurried to catch up to him. "Uncle!" I shouted. He stopped and asked me if my father wanted him back. "No," I said, "he doesn't even know I'm here." "What are you here for then?" He asked, and I told him I wanted to help if I could. He just smiled. I asked his name, and he told that his name was Nyindo, meaning "nose", and that's when I saw his clumsy nose. We sat down and I asked him why my father had chased him away, but he said that he didn't know.

"You're just a child, you wouldn't understand," he added with a gentle voice. I told him that I was sure I would understand and when I looked into his eyes I realised that he wouldn't say anything. I asked him if he wanted to hear my story. He agreed, moving a little closer to me.

"You know, you are not the only one my father doesn't like. He hates me too." I began telling him how I was treated and when my tears stopped me from speaking, he reached out his hands and wiped them away. Then he told me a little about himself and a story about my family. He told me that my grandfather divorced my grandmother and chased away my father, forbidding him ever to come back. At the age of fourteen my father went to live with a chief not far from his father's home. My father was allowed to continue his studies only as long as he worked at the chief's farm. My grandfather remarried and had a son, named Nyindo. A few years later, my grandfather became sick and before he died he left all his riches to his wife and son, but nothing was left to my father. My uncle was too young to manage the documents so they were left in his mother's care.

I asked him why he came begging at my father's if he already had inherited these riches. He said that it was because my father took everything. "When our father died, your father came to the funeral and managed to get the documents from his stepmother." I was very quiet while he talked. After my father got everything he revealed his true colours by chasing my uncle Nyindo and his mother away.

After he finished his story he began to cry. We sat in silence as I tried to find a way to help. Suddenly I remembered my mother and father in Christ. I knew they would understand. I was sure that she was aware of how I was treated by my family and I told my Nyindo I was going to take him to my mother in Christ. He turned and looked at me with a distant hope in his eyes, and when he followed me up the hill I pointed out the house. I saw his tears vanish like a forgotten dream as he hurried to hug me with a smile. While walking I talked about my mother back home, but when I mentioned the word mother for the second time, he interrupted by saying "She's not your mother".I found it hard to believe and I thought he only said this because of some hate he had for them.

My mother in Christ was in her garden with one of her sons, sewing a tablecloth. I was moved by her warm smile as she hurried to welcome us. We were offered milk in her beautiful glasses with flowers on them. I did all the talking, while my uncle prayed for a good reply. I asked her if it was possible for my uncle to sleep at her place for a few days, and she agreed, condemning my father. When I turned my eyes towards him, ready to share a smile of triumph, I was shocked as he was crying again. I did not understand. This time we were on the winning side. I had to say goodbye, though it was hard, and I had to hold my heart for a moment, pretending that everything was okay. I knew somehow that I would never see him again. I left with a broken heart and tears falling like gentle rain.

When I got home, my mother was putting food on the table. My father was home, which meant my mother would give me more food than I could eat. That night it was a perfect match because I could not eat. Every time I looked at my mother and father I felt something squeezing me inside. I looked at my father with a fearful heart because of what he had done to my uncle, and I thought that one day he might chase me away too.

My fear was crazy and out of control. I ran outside and began throwing up. My father followed me. He stood waiting until I had finished, took me by my hand and threw me into the hallway, asking me what I had eaten. I heard my mother's voice in the background, complaining that no matter how much food she gave me I still had things I wasn't supposed to – like mangoes, oranges and bananas. She threatened to leave my father because of me and demanded that he do something about my behaviour. My father's face became like the bulls I used to watch fighting amongst our cows. I closed my eyes. When he pushed me against the wall I thought of telling him that my uncle's tears angered me, but I shut my mouth.

Later that night I went to my bed in the silence of my dark room. Thinking about my uncle's words, all I could feel were the tears running into my mouth.

When I woke up the next morning, I realised that I had been badly beaten. My body hurt and I had dried blood on my nose and mouth. I did not change my bloody clothes because I wanted to make my father feel sorry for me. I went outside, washed my face with cold water and started to sweep the ground in front of our house. The sun had risen, bringing the heat with it. I was getting dizzy. Still, I wanted to try and finish what I had started. I was carried away by thoughts about my uncle and I stopped working when I saw him being strangled by hungry lions.

When I woke up I was lying under the tree in front of the house, covered by a wet blanket. I had no idea how I had come to be there, but I stayed there, hoping my father would come and check on me. But he never did, and I realised again that he didn't care. I threw the blanket aside and sat there for a minute or two, thinking of where I could get something to eat. I told my mother I was going to check on the calves, but she didn't respond, so I left. I headed for the banana plantation and looked for ripe bananas. As I walked between the palm trees I heard the sound of footsteps on dried leaves. I ignored them. I tried very hard not to make any noise and finally I managed to get a bunch of bananas. I had until the sound of footsteps was very close. Then I gathered as many bananas as I could fit in my dress. When I stood up I saw my father talking with three men and it appeared as if they were walking in my direction. I ran as fast as I could, zigzagging between the palm trees like a hunted rabbit.

At the dinner table I looked down at my plate as I heard my father tell his wife what had happened at the banana plantation. I nearly burst into laughter when I heard my mother say, "Maybe they were dogs!"

I could not dry your tears, uncle, when I watched them run like mountain streams. I know that wherever you are, the love and care I tried to give you will always be in your heart.

With my heart I see you in far-off dreams. I believe you also remember me with your open heart, even though I will never know where your soul is. My heart and my eyes lament your sadness. My soul is with you and your words are with me.

Holding onto the Rope

MY MOTHER'S SISTERS OFTEN CAME TO VISIT. While she talked to them she would stare at me. It hurt me because I thought it was her silent way of telling me what a horrible child I was. I could not understand what she meant and her words affected me greatly.

I was troubled by the evil thoughts that formed in my head because of their rejection. My family found no place for me in their hearts.

I had to find a way to cope before I exploded inside. I was getting desperate, having no one who could give me what I wanted. There were so many things missing in my life – I could no longer comprehend why I was there. There was nothing more I wanted on this earth, than to be free, but where could I find the kind of life I wanted? My mother pulled and I pulled, but it never got anywhere. I promised myself I would never give up and let her take away my soul. I would go on pulling and pulling until my hands bled, for I was certain that the rope would break someday

I carried so much pain with me, looking for a sister or a friend so that I could unload the things inside me. There was no one.

I got to the point where I no longer cared how I was treated at home. I only wanted to get out of my present situation. One evening, just after the cows had been milked, Jane arrived to tell my mother she had no one to help her clean where the cows lived. She said she could not make her children do the cleaning because they would be late for school. My mother told Jane she would send me to her in the morning.

I worked in the cowshed for a week before I realised what was happening to my feet. The problem was that I was always too tired to wash myself. The cow's urine had corroded the skin on my feet and although I tried to everything I could to take away the black spots, nothing worked. I even used a stone, but when they bled I left them, and the hatred for my mother's family boiled inside me.

One Saturday afternoon my mother gave me a basket full of bananas which she told me to take to her mother's. When I arrived, the girls counted the bananas and said that I had eaten some. I was upset by this and swore at them calling them poor beings who only came to beg. I told them to stop eating my father's food. The girls started chasing me around, shouting at me as I tried to run as fast as I could, still swearing at them. I told them that if my father had not helped them, they would be dead by now. I heard their cry of surprised anger, and then I headed for home.

My mother was not home and I took a deep breath thinking that now I would get a little time by myself. But when I looked behind me I saw the two girls, still following me. Quickly I ran into the kitchen and took a bunch of bananas and hid under my father's bed, as I expected them to wait for me outside. I started eating the bananas until I could eat no more and my stomach had become so big that I couldn't manage to get out from under the bed. I woke up to my father's voice calling me. At first I thought I was dreaming because he was supposed to be at the town house. I came out from under the bed, and greeted my father. I remembered all the banana skins under the bed, and hoped that nobody would find them. The following day my mother cleaned the house, and she found all the banana skins. To my humiliation, I was the only suspect as all my brothers and sisters were at our grandmother's. My father took my hand and led me straight to the pile of banana skins. We stood in slience before he gave a surprised laugh and shook his head. He demanded I tell him who had eaten the bananas and promised not to beat me. I looked up at him and said "It's the people who live in the bush, with hair all over them." "Did you see them?" he asked, laughing. He laughed so much that he started to cry, and I knew that he didn't believe me.

I told him the girls had been chasing me so hard, so I hid in the bush. When I finally returned home I was so hungry that I ate all the bananas. He didn't say anything and left the room. I heard him talking to his wife in the living room. He told her that he wanted Jane, her mother, to leave his farm. My mother tried to persuade him to change his mind, but he wouldn't listen. My father's anger was getting out of control and I ran to my bedside. I heard her scream from outside.

From the window I could see my mother on the ground, her scream made me cover my ears. But still I wanted him to beat her more. My father left her in bed where she stayed until morning. My father returned in the evening. When I woke up he had already returned to the town house. My mother was in the living room, holding a wet cloth to her face. I went outside and watched the birds flying in the sky. A while later I went down to where Byoma was tying up a couple of goats. When I was sure he hadn't seen me, I went to where he was drying his grasshoppers. I picked at them to make it look like a hen had eaten them and took a handful for myself which I hid.

The next day my mother asked me to make her some tea. I ran to the hen run and began gathering the hen's droppings. I dried my gatherings on the fire while I kept an eye on the door. I took a stone and ground the droppings to a fine powder before mixing them with some tea. I had heard that if people ate chicken droppings they would lose their teeth. I enjoyed watching her drink her tea, and the more she drank, the more my excitement grew. To my disappointment, she didn't lose her teeth.

That evening, when I came back from fetching water, I felt hungry and discovered some food left in the pot. I was about to eat it when I remembered I always had to ask permission to eat, and I stood there for a while doing nothing with my eyes in the pot. I decided to sneak my hands into the pot but even before I took my first bite my mother appeared in the doorway. She squashed the food out of my hand and smashed it in my face. Hurt and angry I ran outside, picked up a stone and started beating the ground, still I wasn't satisfied because she had hurt me so much. I told myself I would not give up before I found a way to punish her.

The next day, when cleaning the house, I found medicine bottles in a box. I took them out to look for one I could use to poison her. While I was choosing what to use, I heard her call my name and in my haste to put the medicine back, I poured it on my dress. It stank like rotten meat. When my mother smelled it, she wrinkled up her nose and before she said anything I explained that I had dropped the medicine box. She screamed at me not to ever go near the medicine box. But her screaming didn't prevent me from trying again.

Later that day she went to check on her children at my grandmother's. I went back to the medicine box and found what we used to give the calves. It had no smell so I thought it wasn't too dangerous. The problem, I realised, was that I couldn't put the medicine in her tea because she put in the milk herself. But I did remember that we ate soft porridge with milk every morning and a perfect idea formed as I remembered this. She returned home later that evening and we ate. While I was doing my chores, I laughed at what I had planned for her.

The morning came with the hot African sun and its blue sky. I was standing by the door like a guard dog waiting to do my morning duty. When the porridge was ready, I put some aside in two cups and went outside to fetch my little bottle of medicine. I mixed it into her porridge in the pot. Then I went to her bedroom and informed her that breakfast was ready. I left her in the living room about to eat her porridge and went outside to eat mine.

Two hours went by without anything happening, but just as I was thinking of what more I could do, I spotted her running as fast as she could to the toilet. I was the happiest child in all the countryside! After a while, when I lost count of her visits to the toilet, I became frightened and thought of telling her – it was only my fear of her wanting to kill me that stopped me. I was like a wet rat. I began to shiver as the sweat ran down her face. I heard her tell me in a calm voice that I should call her a doctor, and I ran to his home as fast as I could.

On my way back I decided to tell the doctor everything I had done. He asked me what kind of medicine I had given her. I told him it was the medicine we give to the calves when their stomachs don't work. After having begged him not to let her know, the doctor looked at me with puzzled eyes and smiled, shaking his head. "What made you do that to her?" He asked. I told him everything about my family, and I saw his eyes become bigger and bigger. I was afraid. I folded my arms and began walking around the house, hoping to get rid of my increasing fear. I was beginning to hate myself for what I had done. The doctor came back to me. "You must never do that again, do you hear?" He warned.

"Yes," I replied in a small, frightened voice. "Will she die?"

"No," he replied, "did you want her to die?" Before leaving, he guaranteed me that she would live and everything would be all right. When I couldn't see him anymore, I began to cry but I didn't know why.

When she first came to live with us my stepmother appeared to be sincere, and she seemed to have good intentions. Later on however, I observed her empty promises. She was thirsty for my blood, although death was nothing compared to what she had planned for me. I seemed to be the only thing standing in her way.

The Truth about Mother

LATER THAT YEAR MY FATHER CAME TO VISIT THE FARM. In the morning he sent me to fetch the men who slaughtered cows. I returned an hour later and my father was standing outside. Immediately he took over and showed them the cow, but I was afraid to watch animals being killed, so I busied myself with clearing the leaves from the garden. By the time I was told to take the dishes for the meat, the men had already finished. It didn't take them much time before they had a fire, and I stood there watching the men going wild. One was boiling the intestines while the other struggled with the cow's head. It didn't take a minute before he had the cow's tongue in his hands. He looked at it with such longing that it seemed like he might eat it raw.

A few hours later the guests arrived. One of the four men had skin the colour of light. I watched the man, sure that I had never seen that kind of person before. I tried to get close to him to see if it was the fire that made him look so different to us. I loved the way he looked with his big and shiny dark brown eyes and tall body, with a moustache under his big nose. I wanted to reach out and touch him, thinking that if I pinched his skin it would come off in my hands. But because my father was there, I did not try it.

I imagined another world with no beatings – a world in which I would not be told how and when to eat.

When I thought of this other world my tears began to run like a stream, and my head became too heavy for me. I went to sit near our big tree, watching the visitors enjoy themselves. In the evening the guests left, leaving me with a lot to clean and while I was busy, father walked over to me. He told me he would take me to the town house the following day, and with a smile he handed me a present. I felt utter joy and my headache was suddenly forgotten. I stood there smiling, not knowing what to do. I was relieved when my mother took him away. I went to bed that evening with a clear mind, and my dreams were light and happy.

The next morning, as we arrived at the town house, three girls and a boy were staring at me – my father told me they were my sisters and my brother. I stared at them, noticing their fine clothes, which made them look weak and spoiled. They were curious about me and asked how our stepmother treated me. I didn't know the word "stepmother", so I just looked back at their faces, waiting for an explanation. "Mutesi," they said.

"Do you mean our mother?" I asked.

"No!" they protested. "That woman is not our mother."

"Then where is our mother?" I asked. They had no idea where she was.

I began telling them how badly she treated me. They looked sad and I asked them how they were. "Does she mistreat you whenever she comes here?" They replied no. I went away and sat alone for a moment to think things over. I thought back to my mother's abuse of me and still I found my heart too weak to accept the fact that she was not my real mother. In silence I decided to change her name from "mother" to "stepmother".

After two days yet another one of my sisters, Annette, arrived at the house. Annette was our oldest sister from another woman. I accepted her just as I did my other brothers and sisters. Her presence bothered my sisters except for Grace, my sister by my real mother. She was a quiet person who was brave and had a determined heart. She would fight to the death if anything threatening crossed her path, and I often created fights between her and Margie who always bossed us around and wanted us to live by her rules. One day I heard my sisters talking about Annette and I couldn't work out why they needed to do it.

I just saw Annette cry every day without being able to help or do anything and I was relieved whenever Marie, our nanny, comforted her. The new surroundings suited me fine. I got along with my brother Richard, and Marie showed me that not all women were bad. It was 1982, and my sisters went back to boarding school. I started my first year at a Catholic school called the Uganda Martyrs where my brother Richard, my real mother's fourth child, was at school. I was angry with Richard because he gave me trouble at school because he had introduced me as "Baby". Everyone seemed to love that name except me. Almost every single day I got new bruises fighting children who called me Baby.

One Friday, my father went to his wife on the farm, leaving my brother and I in Marie's care for the weekend. But as evening approached, she went out with her friends and didn't return. By noon the following day she still hadn't returned. Then we realised the tremendous freedom we had without any adults around.

Behind the town house my father had a little piece of land with green bananas, called *matoke*, and other fruit and vegetables. We took as many banana leaves as we could carry to the market and sold them. With our money we bought tasty, sweet bananas and ate them while gazing at the busy crowd of people going about their business.

Once we had eaten our fill, we went to the next stand and bought more bananas. We carried on like that for a long time, feeling wild with freedom. Suddenly I felt a strange sensation in my stomach. We had used up all our money when the noise in my stomach began. I spun around and looked at the woman who had been selling us the banana to see if she heard the noise. I began pulling my brother towards the nearest exit, as he struggled to get the last bananas into his pockets. Panicking, I asked him if there were any toilets nearby, but he only laughed. I started running towards the only toilet I knew in the area, at my school, but I was too late.

Before I reached my empty school I had left a trail of embarrassment, I gave up on the race with my stomach, walking slowly to make sure that nothing else would leave my body. I left the toilet feeling relieved and disappointed. My brother refused to lend me his shirt, so on our way home my brother walked on the street while I had to sneak through the bush trying to hide my bare bottom.

Marie was relieved when she saw us and hurried to cover me up.

When my father and his wife came back with my stepsisters and brothers, she had with her a little baby called Godwin Mwesigye. I had to take care of him every day after school. I had no time to play or fight and I was so angry that I almost threw the baby in the privy, except I knew that if I did I would never get to play again. Instead I started finding other ways to escape babysitting.

One day I was sitting in front of the house with him in my arms, watching all the others play. They had been calling me several times to come and join them so I became angry and pinched him on the thumb. He cried and cried, and he made me afraid that his mother might see the bruise. I hoped my stepmother would come to get her child, but she didn't. I thought that if I made the baby scream his mother would come and relieve me.

This time I had to pinch him on the back. Finally, after a few more pinches my plan worked. My stepmother came running towards us and grabbed her child. But again she proved to be too mean and clever for me. She gave me the job of washing all her baby's nappies. I had become the joke of the neighbourhood! But the more they laughed, the angrier I became. I hated all of them. Every time I had the opportunity I picked a fight with a child. There was one child I didn't pick on – my friend Sofia, who never made jokes about me.

One day when I found shit in the nappies, I decided that it looked like scrambled eggs. I went inside the house and added a little bit of salt and gave it to my stepbrothers, Ray and Emanuel. I was thrilled when they asked for more, but I told them to wait until tomorrow. Still, I hoped that my sisters would return so they could take over my duties.

A week or two passed before all of them came home from boarding school. I was so excited about getting time off. Now the town house was crowded and my stepmother was upset about it. She was always sick, spending most of her time in bed, and when she didn't she would manipulate my father into beating my sisters. This is probably why Annette and Grace became good friends, spending most of their time together. One Saturday morning, Annette and Grace disappeared. Later that day my father searched for them, but he returned home alone. When they left I hoped more than ever that my father would see what kind of a person my stepmother was.

Impossible Fight

WHEN MY STEPMOTHERS' CHILDREN started school, they each had two pairs of shoes, while I didn't even have a single dress. I asked her to buy me one – she only told me to ask my father. In the evening, I went to the living room where he was sitting with a pipe in his hands. When he looked at me I noticed an unusual smile which made me feel brave, so I told him what I wanted. His smile remained, telling me that he would buy me a beautiful dress. I hardly slept that night, lying in my bed with butterflies in my stomach, trying to figure out what the dress would look like.

The following day, when I spotted my father returning from work, I hurried to greet him and carried the parcel and his briefcase inside. I went to the living room where I stood with the parcel in my hands until my father told to open it. To my disappointment it was a black dress with two white stripes on the chest. But it wasn't the stripes that bothered me. It had a very low-cut chest and back, but I didn't dare tell him how disappointed I was. I was too scared that my old father would give me a new round of beatings. Instead I ran outside to hide. I cried, wishing the dress off my body. My sister Margie followed and told me I looked beautiful in it, and that it was the latest fashion. But what she didn't realise was that I didn't care that it was in fashion. I hated it because I felt naked in it. I have never forgotten that dress. I still dream of it as part of my impossible fight to cover myself against unwanted eyes.

I went to school in that long dress and bare feet, while my stepsister and brother had everything they desired. Fortunately, the days went by quietly, I was tormented only by my own worry. On my way home one day, I was walking with a lowered head, trying to avoid the stones that cut my feet. I was trying to think of a lie to make my father buy me a pair of shoes. I didn't think that the sharp stones would be a good reason.

Before I got home I met Sofia, who went to Newton Nursery School. I told her about my burning desire to have shoes. She told me to tell my father the school would refuse to let me in again without shoes. I smiled, knowing he would then have to buy them for me.

I got what I wanted, but I never got what my stepsister and brother had. But it didn't matter. I was soon saved because our school later decided we had to wear a school uniform. I was overjoyed.

At the break times I would hide in the woods until it was over because I felt bad watching my stepsister and brother buy whatever they desired. If I stayed at the school, I would have to see them getting more than what they could finish. They were selfish, always looking the other way, as though I had my own treats. They never shared anything with me. But I couldn't hate them – I knew they behaved like that because their mother wanted to fill their hearts with greed.

I began to think my worries would never end. I was still bothered by children at school because of the way I was dressed. My stepbrother and sister had more than three uniforms each while I had one that had to last the whole week. The children at my school didn't know we had different mothers. When they asked me questions about my uniform I felt embarrassed, afraid of what might happen if I answered them, so I just looked down or walked away. I don't remember what made me break the silence one day. I didn't know what this would do.

One day when I got to school, Baryareba, one of my friends, was waiting for me with a pair of shoes. She told me to try them on. I was thrilled, as they fitted my feet perfectly. I was shy, not knowing how to thank her. Despite my happiness I wanted to take them off and put on my old shoes, but my friend didn't let me.

When I got home, my stepmother looked at me with frightened eyes, and asked me where I had stolen the shoes. With sad eyes I told her that I hadn't stolen them, that my friend had given them to me. She was angry and shouted at me. "You're begging from people as if you had no father!" She then told me she would tell my father. During supper everyone except me seemed to enjoy the meal. I stared at my stepmother. After she told my father about the shoes he turned like a dog disturbed by flies.

"What?" My father roared, standing up and ordering me to bring both pairs. Carrying the shoes he told me to follow him, and when we reached the privy, he grabbed my hand and said, "Look!" and threw them in.

After I had cried many tears I went to bed and thought about my sisters who had gone back to boarding school. The morning brought rain, but I couldn't wait and ran through the rain, protecting myself with a banana leaf.

When I told my friends about the night before, I cried even harder when I saw they felt sorry for me. One of the girls, who most of us saw as our leader, said she and the other girls should tell their parents about the shoes. The next day after school my friends' parents were standing next to a car in the school compound, waiting for me.

One of the fathers greeted me and I went limp when he told me they would try to reason with my father. When we were almost home, I got so afraid that no matter how much I tried to squeeze my legs together I couldn't hold it in. My father was standing in the garden with his hands in his pockets.

When I got out of the car I was confused about where I should stand so I froze, looking into my father's eyes hoping he would tell me what to do. He said nothing, so I went and stood by his side.

The man said hello and then told him that I was his daughter's friend and that I had got the shoes from her.

My father wasn't interested, and I could tell what he was going to say just by looking at his face. "Go away – all of you!" The men who I thought would fight for me left without doing anything. My father turned on me as if he was a hungry lion, though I seemed too big for him to swallow. After spitting me out, he left me on the ground and went into the house. That evening I overheard that my stepmother was going back to the farm. I got excited and my sadness disappeared.

Part Two

Into the Fire

Hunted

IN 1982, MILTON OBOTE'S GOVERNMENT was under siege. At the time, he believed the rebels in Uganda, the National Resistance Army (NRA), were supported by Tutsis and those people living in western Uganda.

When he decided to act on his ideas, his government urged the entire population to chase the Tutsis out of Uganda. Obote probably believed the only solution to end rebel attacks would be to send all Tutsis back to Rwanda. In fact, what he didn't realise was that he himself was the problem in Uganda. I am not sure if he was really trying to find a solution to the problem because he was power thirsty, just like many other leaders in Africa who are only concerned with their own well-being, and who always have problems with their pockets, which carry too many holes.

However, Obote didn't understand that by sending the Tutsis back to the country that had butchered them was not the best way to stay in power. He met with more and more resistance from the strong NRA. The Tutsis looked at where Obote was sending them and they saw death. I do not suppose that death itself worried them, but their terror lay in the way in which they would die. The Tutsis were terrified of dying at the hands of Obote's men, and many of them tried to join the NRA. Officially, Obote was doing everything in the name of peace and stability. Obote's neighbours did not object to his actions, possibly because other African leaders used similar tactics on a smaller scale and would not have been able to condemn him without raising serious questions about their own regimes. All they did was to carry on in their own ways, filling their stomachs. The Tutsis suffered just like the Indians under Idi Amin.

My family was also of Tutsi origin, and that was the beginning of my family's endless pain. Many Ugandans were against sending the Tutsis back to Rwanda. Even though the Government was behind it, Ugandans tried to save what they could. My mother and father came to Uganda in the 1950s and we had all been born in Uganda.

I watched what was happening to the other Tutsi families. I was glad to think that the same would happen to my father and his wife, and that revenge would be mine. But that happiness could not make me forget one incident that still scares me today. The chief of the village abused me and he threatened to kill me if I told anyone about it.

Even now it's so hard for me to think about that evening when that old man dragged me into a deserted, bombed building. And even then I knew there would be more of these experiences. I knew this because I was never able to trust anyone enough to tell them about things I had to face.

Every day it felt as though someone made me think about how I would be tormented the next time and the next, and the next, until I couldn't take it anymore.

When my father heard that the government wanted to chase the Tutsis out of Uganda, he went to the farm to save what he could. On his way he met one of his workers who himself was a Tutsi and who warned him against going to the farm. I was in the garden playing with my friend, Sofia, when I looked up at the road and saw my father with a bag in his hands followed by another man. It made me realise that things on our farm were getting worse, and I was aware of the fact that many of our neighbours didn't like my father. My father had a big piece of land, with a couple of hills and lovely views over beautiful streams. The Ugandans fought over this land. They all behaved like hungry lions, and even those he once helped turned against him. They were the first to slaughter his cows and goats.

The Ugandans looted the houses while others went down to the fields and slashed the banana plants down to the ground as they were shouting, "No Tutsis must ever return or they will be killed!"

Our neighbours' hearts were like those of my own family and they took advantage of the situation. They took my father's cows from their new-born calves; the calves died of hunger because they could no longer suckle at their mothers, and the cows were slaughtered because they tried to return to their calves.

They searched for my father on his land and in his house, and when they didn't find him, they made sure that the two houses were burned to the ground. My father's pride was taken away and his bitterness knew no bounds. I was concerned about the goats, and I hoped to hear that my grandmother and stepmother had lost their arms or legs.

When my father heard about the destruction of his farm he seemed totally confused. I saw him going round and round the house with one hand in his pocket and the other on his head, looking at the ground as though it would help him understand it all. I saw him go back inside, sit on the sofa and cry.

From the window I watched my father smashing everything in the living room, talking to himself the whole time.

A few days later my sisters returned from school, and were taken to one of my father's friends. My brother and I went with him to the new farm and I could see tears of anger in my father's eyes. He took out all his desperation on us. The journey got longer and longer, and it really felt as if we were driving into hell – every time I turned to look at him, he spat into my face.

He told us a lot about the people who had stolen his riches. I could not understand why, if he were so wise – with all his books and learning and property, he couldn't be kind and understanding to his children?

He kept on swearing at my mother, even though she wasn't there, saying, "Stupid woman! She only produced girls, no boys. Now I am alone because of all of you girls!"

I was puzzled by his words. What about the four sons he got through his new wife? My hope grew stronger as my father's weakened. In a moment of weakness he had mentioned my real mother!

The new place was not as perfect as the old farm with its banana plantation. My grandmother was already there, and without bothering to ask us of our journey, she began telling her son that some of his cows had run away to the old farm. My father turned and slapped me hard. I saw stars as I fell to the ground. I felt a sharp pain in my stomach when he began kicking me, and he carried on kicking me until I heard our veterinarian shout at him. I got up and went into the house to rinse my mouth. I was disappointed to see the woman I hated most standing there watching. "Here we go again," I said to myself. "Am I ever going to be free of this woman?"

My Dark Side

ON OUR WAY TO WHERE THE CALVES were grazing, I asked my brother what we should do when we weren't given food. He turned and looked straight at me, and said, "In the morning, when we take the goats to graze, we'll make sure that we bring the dogs too. We'll make them kill one of the goats and then we'll have something to eat." I looked at him with troubled eyes because to me it sounded like a brutal act. I told him about my love for the goats and that I would hate the person who laid a hand on them.

But then he replied, "Can't you see that our stepmother and father hate us? So why then do you love their goats?" I looked down for a moment. "Maybe it's just that they are animals. Let's not make them bleed for our father's mistakes." I saw him smile, and it seemed to me that I had changed his mind.

Our father and his wife went back to the town house, leaving us with our grandmother, taking my two worst worries with them, though they left us without proper food. Life on the farm became harder – we had to live on milk and *posho* every day, and if there was no posho our meals consisted of milk only.

Each morning we told her that we loved to drink our milk outside. We would then take the dogs' plates behind the house and give the dogs our milk. We would wait for them to finish before going back inside. Our dogs became fat and were better looking than the neighbour's dogs. Our plan was working perfectly until one day when the dogs started fighting for the milk, making so much noise that she came to see what was going on. She screamed at us, saying that one day we would remember the milk we had given to the dogs. Her words caught my attention, and I thought of what she could have meant. Her words made me shake inside.

It got worse when my brother told her that we needed something else to eat and mentioned a hen. She told us that we were nothing but murderers who wanted to eat everything, even with our father still living. She became almost hysterical, saying that when our father died there would be nothing left because of us because we wanted to kill and eat everything. She made it clear nothing belonged to us, and we should forget about inheriting anything. I felt my fear and anger and told myself to destroy as much as I could. I didn't care about anything that belonged to my father. I knew I had nothing to lose, and it didn't worry me that lions had his cows.

Early one morning, while walking with the goats, my brother and I talked to each other about our grandmother's words. When we got to some bush far away from any unwanted eyes, we sent the dogs after one of the goats. The dogs caught a young goat by its leg. We provoked it to keep on biting the goat. I felt no remorse when it began to cry in fear and pain – I saw it as part of my father.

The following day heavy rain prevented us from taking the goats to graze. My grandmother and I were sitting by the fire while my brother relaxed on his bed. The sound of heavy rain silenced us. Then I saw the wounded goat in the doorway. It was soaked and stood there shaking for a while before it limped over to my brother's bed. As it crawled under the bed, my brother reached for its mouth and nose and I went there to help him as it fought for its life. My grandmother just sat there with her old back staring at us. The goat gave up its desperate fight, and we ran to our grandmother. When we told her that the goat was about to die she looked pleased and told my brother to take it outside and slaughter it.

Remembering how the goat had struggled to live I became more and more afraid. It was then that I told myself that the only way I could rid myself of my fear was to kill other creatures. I knew a boy nearby and I was certain he knew how to kill a cow because his father was a butcher. One fine evening I went with one of the dogs to the boy's home. He told me that every evening before I went to bed I should put a peace of meat on a stick and make the cow smell it for ten minutes. He said that after about five days the cow would die. I did as he had said and on the fourth day I was very excited. I ran out to find the dead cow. To my disappointment she was there playing with the others, and seemed stronger than ever. I thought that perhaps I hadn't followed his instructions properly.

One morning I wasn't feeling well, and my brother had to take the goats on his own. I waited for him the whole day. At around six o'clock in the evening he returned with tired eyes.

When the foreman had finished counting the goats, he found one missing and he went to tell my grandmother. She arrived, screaming so loudly that even the dogs shivered. She went straight to my brother and started to beat him. The dogs sat watching, their worried eyes looking from one side to the other. I was leaning against the wall, feeling angry as she hit his head into the ground. But then the dogs couldn't stand it any longer and jumped in to save their friend.

Two of the dogs jumped on her and started tearing at her clothes until the skirt was ripped off her body (thank God she had something on underneath).

The next morning, she wouldn't give the dogs anything to eat or drink. She warned us that if we tried to steal milk for them, we would not eat. But we knew a lot of tricks so that our beloved long-eared dogs wouldn't go hungry. When I got older I understood a little about why my grandmother was like this. She had no other relatives except her son – my father, and a daughter. Her daughter lived far from us, and she never visited her mother. I still wonder what happened to her relatives.

One evening my brother and I returned from one of our rabbit hunts and found our stepmother at the house.

Two days later my father also arrived. In the evening he called the workers for a meeting where he told the two of them to find another job because he could no longer afford to pay them. While eating supper my father told my brother and I to get ready – we were moving to the town house.

When we arrived I couldn't find Margie or Helen, and when I asked Marie, she told me that they were at boarding school. My brother and I had a week in which to settle down. My brother met up with his old pals again and I saw all my old enemies. A few days passed before I learned that my old friends who had been there in my first year at school had gone. I felt very lonely.

I found it hard to make friends because I often wanted to be on my own. However, I was lucky and a week later made friends with two sisters from the third grade. Judith and Mutton were dressed so smartly with the latest shoes, and they always carried lots of pocket money. Everyone respected them and I could see that only specially chosen people could be their friends.

I had chosen them, not the other way round, so they never seemed that interested in me. But they let me hang around them. One day their mother came to our school. As we talked she asked my father's name. She knew him and to my surprise, she had also known my real mother.

Her kind words caught my attention and, unlike her daughters, she seemed to take a real interest in me. I dared to ask her if she knew where my mother was, but she only smiled and went away.

The woman had introduced herself as Patricia, and gave me her address but repeatedly warned me not to show it to my father. I hid the address and even forgot to show it to my sisters when they came home for the holidays.

My sister Margie surprised us all with the strength of a real woman. She fought my stepmother relentlessly. My stepmother grew thinner every day, still, she managed to create a stand-off between my father and his daughters. I watched my sisters being beaten nearly every day, though Margie only got stronger. Whenever the beatings started Helen would scream, telling him to stop, but Margie would grit her teeth until the beating was over. On occasion I would hear her say, "Father, again you beat me for nothing." One very painful memory was seeing my stepmother moving the furniture away to give my father more room for the beatings.

An Innocent Betrayal

HELEN, OUR OLDEST SISTER, could no longer take my father's beatings. She was tall and well built, light in colour with big shiny brown eyes that made her look very innocent. Helen became a spy, telling our stepmother everything we said and did. She was desperately searching for a way to escape the beatings and her pain blinded her – she didn't realise the evil intentions of the woman who hated us all.

We could not understand how our stepmother came to know our secrets. I told them I had no idea who was giving our secrets away. Margie thought it was our younger stepsister, but I disagreed.

One day Margie suggested we go and steal some bananas from one of our neighbour's field. When we got there I was told to climb one of the trees with large fruit called *fenne*. One of my sisters was struggling with a stick of sugar cane, while Helen was pulling down a ripe banana plant. I forgot about the fenne and just stayed up in the tree, watching my sisters tearing the trees and plants apart like wild pigs.

Suddenly I heard Margie shout, "Run!"

"Why?" I asked, but they had already fled like a wind. I had one fenne in my hands, and I was ready to drop it to the ground. "Get down, you thief!" When I looked down it was the old woman that we feared so much. She had a big stick in her hands and was looking up into the tree. I noticed that she had no idea of who I was. I kept on telling her that I was getting down while searching for my target. When I saw her head I let the fennel go and the woman fell to the ground. I quickly climbed down, grabbed the fennel and joined my sisters in our little secret place.

When they saw the fenne on top of my head both Margie and Helen laughed. Helen asked me how I had managed to escape. I told her I first had to kill the old woman. They gave me a huge fright when both of them screamed in terror. I watched them in amazement as they turned and ran back to the where the old woman had found me. I followed them but of course, there was no dead body.

A few weeks after the incident with the fenne I began to miss the bananas. I had a good eye for bananas hanging above our kitchen, and that day they were as ripe as they could be. The whole day my mind was occupied in finding out how I could get to them. In the evening I left while everybody was still eating, and went outside to the kitchen. I picked up a long piece of firewood and pushed at a bunch until four of them came down. I went behind the house and had them. The stars were so beautiful that night that I just stared at them. Enjoying the night air and my bananas transported me far away to a perfect world.

But then Helen appeared like lightening and destroyed the peace, flinging me back into reality by calling my name. "Here I am!" I answered without hiding what I had in my hands because I thought she might also want one. "What are you doing?"

"I'm eating a banana," I replied in a whisper. "Do you want one?" I continued, but she refused, telling me she was taking me to my father.

I just smiled because I was certain that she was trying to scare me. A second later I realised she was serious, as I heard her voice again, rumbling at me. This time my reply was true and clear: "Helen, we have the same mother, please don't take me inside." I was begging her, crying and holding her hand, but she refused, and dragged me along. I tried to hold onto the wall using one hand but my fingers were weak trying to accept my sister's betrayal.

Soon I was standing in front of my father. Our stepmother began to cry, telling my father that he didn't appreciate anything she did. She became hostile to my father and as her tears of lies increased, my father got more and more angry. Suddenly he exploded, dragging me onto the floor. Pinning me down with his foot on my shoulder he demanded my reasons for stealing the bananas, except I could not answer him because I knew for sure that my answer would be misunderstoodand and would only add fuel to my stepmother's fire. The beatings didn't seem to please his wife enough, and I saw him look at her quickly before continuing with my punishment.

Then he went to their bedroom, bringing out one of his coats and ordering me to sleep on it. As he put it on my bed he looked at me with a warning in his eyes and told me that the punishment would continue in the morning if I wet it. I was crying as I lay down, not because of the beatings but because I was always expected to do the impossible. I tried to sing to myself to keep myself awake.

In the morning I woke up with a pounding heart as I felt the coat, but there was no coldness, and with refreshed hope I brought it up to my nose. I smelt a strong poison that reminded me of the beating from the day before. I became afraid when I touched my unhealed wounds and I thought of running away, only I didn't know where to go. Then I remembered who had started it all and how sad I was. On my way through the living room I bumped into Helen and stopped for a moment, as I burned with hate for her. I walked outside and sat in the garden to wait for my father.

Finally he appeared, and without a word I brought the coat to him. He stood there a while with his eyes looking at the ground like a thief, and then he called for his big stick. I looked straight at him while my tears ran down into my mouth. I saw shame in his eyes and could not tell whether he was smiling or about to cry. He blinked his eyes continuously. I kept on looking at him with my small eyes until he slowly turned away and walked back to the house.

That very afternoon, Margie and I called Helen to our meeting place. Margie told her we all were fighting for the same thing and that nothing could stop our stepmother from hating us, and that if we betrayed one another, she would only laugh at us. When Helen started crying, Margie and I walked away leaving her on her own with her tears. Later Helen followed us to the potato field and when we were about to dig up some sweet potatoes, she stood in front of us and crossed her heart, promising never to betray any of us again.

The Trade

THE FOLLOWING MORNING, which was a Saturday, my sisters and I were in the garden relaxing in the shade, when we heard the sound of a car. We pricked up our ears like dogs about to go in search of their prey. We looked up at the road and saw our sister Annette, whom we hadn't seen since she ran away. She was in the front seat of an over-crowded Landrover, waving at us from the window. We all screamed, calling her name and running to the road. We couldn't wait for the car to stop before opening the car door. One of my sisters cried, and with a smile on her face Annette managed to get out of the car unhurt.

She had a beautiful little baby girl, named Maculate, in her arms. We all fought to hold the child. When our father heard our shouts and screams, he came outside and stood in front of the house with his pipe between his teeth. When the visitors started walking down towards him he told us to get chairs from the house. At the door we met our step-mother sneaking a fearful look at what was going on. Soon the visitors introduced themselves, and among them was a man with a long nose like a telephone wire. He stood up and presented himself as Mugabo. He said he was there to marry Annette. My father told Mugabo he would have to bring seven cows and four goats to him.

The man told our father that he could only afford four cows and two goats. Our father accepted the offer with an excited smile on his face. In the evening, the visitors left to get the cows and Annette stayed with us. The next weekend my brother-in-law brought the cows and took Annette with him. Even at my age and with my lack of under-standing I worked out that my stepsister didn't love Mugabo. He was almost as old as our father.

After Annette had gone back, our father started telling my sisters and I of how Annette was so special, and he was never sure whether he would get anything from us. Each time we drank milk he would say, "Remember – you are drinking milk from Annette's cows!" It was the song he sang every day. I looked at him and asked myself, "Is he mad or just greedy? Does he want us to get married so young?"

I couldn't work out what disease of the mind my father had. Margie and Helen were bothered by his words, only there was nothing they could do to stop his madness.

Annette never got what she wanted. Her marriage ended and her two children were sent away to her husband's family after the divorce.

One day, our stepmother sent Helen to buy meat for lunch, but she returned without it. Before anybody saw her she went to tell Margie what had happened. She had lost the money. Crying, she asked Margie what she should do. Later, Margie called Richard and I and suggested that we go and beg for money in the streets. After hours of begging we had very little money. Margie told her she had no choice but to tell our stepmother. Helen followed Margie's advice and we heard our stepmother shouting at her, "What do you want me to do? Wait till I tell your father!" Helen cried, begging her not to let our father know.

When he returned and Helen told him what had happened, he slapped her face and said the lost money was there to pay her school fees. My sister knelt on the floor and begged him for forgiveness, but he didn't listen. The following morning my father ordered her to work in the banana plantation near the town house. While the rest of us prepared for school, Helen was looking for the hoe.

Some days passed, but nothing was said. My sister continued working as if the incident was forgotten, but one day when we came back from school Helen was gone. Still my father's face remained unchanged. "Your sister is stupid, just like your mother who is selling onions, and no matter how cheaply she sells them, no one wants to buy them." He continued by telling us that it meant nothing to him if we all ran away, and I had to realise that he hated us just as he hated our mother.

I tried to understand where our lives were heading. I could see that we would probably all go the same way.

Now I was left with one sister and a brother, realising that we had nothing and no one on our side. We saw that our stepmother was not going to give up, so we tried to be careful with everything we did.

The Last Holiday

OUR SCHOOL CLOSED DOWN FOR THE HOLIDAYS and my father took us to the farm where we would spend the holidays with Grandmother.

On our way my father had a short conversation with Richard, telling him that he was now a big boy who should take care of us. My sister and I looked at each other. When we reached the farm, the workers had already slaughtered a cow. We quickly unpacked while the workers made a fire. Then we were told to find ourselves wooden sticks and help ourselves to the meat. Two workers were roasting the animal's kidney, but all three of them wanted to eat it. I felt the tension in the air. One of the workers waited until the kidney was cooked, grabbed it, and ran away, followed closely by the others. He was eating it as he ran but suddenly dropped to the ground without a word. We laughed at first but were interrupted by his pursuers cries and realised that the man on the ground was dead with half a kidney lying beside him. The dead man was wrapped in a blanket and my father said we could not go on with the feast. I was angry at the dead man because he had ruined the feast for us.

My brother told us we should search for honey. Margie told us to get plastic bags to protect us from the bees. Equipped with matches and a hoe we started out, following the light of the moon.

We searched for a while until we found a beehive and began digging. The bees went wild. Some of them got into the plastic bags. In desperation we tried to make enough smoke to calm the bees down and we were covered in sweat after the struggle. And after all that we discovered we couldn't eat the honey because it already had young bees in it.

We returned home and found our grandmother cooking milk at the fire. She turned her angry face towards us. After we drank the milk we said good night and went to bed. In the morning Margie helped the workers to milk the cows while my brother and I watched the calves. Later we went on a rabbit hunt with our five dogs. We caught one rabbit. After roasting the rabbit, I watched the others fighting over the meat, but I wasn't worried about it as I only enjoyed the hunt and not eating the meat. While they ate, we talked about our lack of clothes and my brother suggested selling a cow. Margie said we should rather sell the milk. When we got home, the old woman was standing with a stick in her hands. "Where have you been the whole day?" she yelled. Margie just walked past her. I stood there because I knew her well and was more afraid. She took her breasts in her hands and said to Margie, "These are the breasts I fed your father with and I condemn you with them." Grandmother told Margie she would die wandering the roads before being eaten by vultures. I just looked at her and shook my head. My sister seemed to ignore her words and she laughed loudly from inside the house.

The following day we decided to carry out our plan of selling some milk to buy clothes. By nine o'clock we had filled a can of milk and taken it to the main road. There we sold it to a truck driver and gave the money to Margie. The following morning she caught a taxi to town. We waited the whole day for her to return. When she finally came home she was wearing high heels and a fine dress. We asked her for our clothes and instead she gave us sweets and cakes saying that there wasn't enough money for our clothes. We were angry and said we would tell our grandmother that she had sold the milk. We saw the terror in her eyes but we didn't care. She asked for forgiveness but we went straight to Grandmother and told her. She instructed one of the workers to go and tell our father. I felt bad and told Margie that I didn't know it would go that far. And as I thought about our sisters Helen and Grace I began to cry.

We begged Margie to stay and promised to tell our father that we had lied to Grandmother.

But Margie decided to leave us anyway. She couldn't live with our stepmother and grandmother's harsh rules.

Our holiday was over and it was time for us to return to the town house. When we arrived, our stepmother had a huge smile on her face that was larger than normal. I guessed it was because Margie had left. Our stepmother seemed to be winning her war because our nanny also seemed tired of my stepmother's new rules. When Margie decided to leave we all wept, begging her to stay because she was the only person who loved us.

Marie saw us crying and promised not to leave. In the morning breakfast was there on the table. After eating we went to say goodbye to Marie – we always said goodbye before going to school, but she wasn't home. We went to the banana plantation not far from the house, thinking that she might be down there, but she was nowhere to be found. On our way to school we talked about the things she had done for us. It made us sad that she wasn't there but we just hoped she would be home when we returned. Now Marie was gone too, and in order to go on, even though I felt destroyed, I had to strengthen myself and face my pain without fear. I decided to pretend that nothing had disturbed me.

Now only my brother and I were at home to cope with our stepmother. The problem was that he and I didn't see things the same way, so it was hard to count on him.

It was about four o'clock in the afternoon on a Thursday, and I had nothing to do, so I went to watch the rich men play golf. I was sitting with my head in my hands when a man called Johnson approached me. He suggested I help him to carry golf bags. "Sure!" I responded without a second thought because I knew that I would get some money for doing this. After working with him he gave me more money than I expected, enough to keep me happy for days. I was so exited I forgot all the troubles that usually haunted me, and I walked home feeling on top of the world because I had something to show at school, just like all the other children.

When I got home my stepmother wasn't there. When she returned she didn't bother to ask of where I had been. I supposed she was still pleased about Margie's disappearance. Early in the morning I got up and did what I was supposed to do, and then hurried to school before anyone woke up. On my way I stopped at one of the stands that was owned by a man whom we used to call "Monkey". I bought some bananas and had them as I continued my journey to school.

Before I got to school I bought three packets of sweets and stuffed them in my school bag. During break I gave my classmates as many sweets as they could eat, but we couldn't finish them and we came back to class, some of us still chewing on them. The teacher asked which one of us had bought the sweets and all the children looked at me. When the teacher wasn't looking, I silently tried to make them shut up. When no one answered, she told those whom she'd caught to stand in front of the class. She called Kayirangwa and told him to bring some sticks inside. When they heard this, they broke the silence and told her I had bought the sweets. The teacher told me to see her before going home.

After class she gave me a letter to give to my father. I looked nervously at the letter and she told me that he was being called to a meeting at the school. On my way home, I sat by the roadside and tried to read it but I couldn't read the difficult handwriting. At home my father was drinking beer and talking legal things with another man. When I handed him the letter he put it in his pocket. When the visitor had gone, he called me and asked what I had done. "Nothing," I replied. He told me he would find out the following day anyway. My heart beat faster and faster, as I thought the teacher had probably told him about the sweets.

The night seemed shorter than usual and morning came too quickly. When I got to school my teacher asked me about my father, and with burning hatred I told her that he would be coming in soon. At the morning parade everyone except me was at prayers.

Just as the prayers ended my father arrived, and I had to concentrate on not wetting my pants. He walked past us to where the teachers were standing and spoke to them. Then he called my name and ordered me to stand in front of everyone. My father started telling everyone that I was a thief and had stolen his money and used it to buy sweets. All eyes were on me and I felt my shame like a thief. He asked one of the teachers for a stick and ordered me to lie down on my stomach. I remained standing and I thought of telling everyone how I was treated at home, but before I could decide, he grabbed my neck and forced me to the ground.

I struggled to get up, telling him that I wanted to tell the truth. He stopped the whipping and I stood up, wondering whether the teachers would help me or not.

I looked into his eyes and lay down on the ground. When I tried to see how the other children felt, I noticed that most of them looked the other way, some even cried. When he had left, my teacher asked me if the man who had been beating me was my real father. Without a word I turned away, and in silence I wished he would die and go to hell. During break time I noticed that most of the children looked at me with sad eyes. They all wanted to be my friend, and that day, Judith and Mutton gave me all their goodies. At home my father demanded to know where I had got the money, so I told him the truth. My shameless father was about to whip me the second time when we were interrupted by a visitor.

That day I realised all my father's power came from others' pain.

A Path of Fear

LIFE WAS A GREAT STRUGGLE FOR ME THEN. I was constantly fighting for my sanity while my stepmother didn't stop her cruel treatment of us. Word had even spread to distant homes of a father beating his children at their stepmother's command. For a while I was the only victim, and my brother escaped punishment.

One day, with a smile on her face, she told me she was sending me with her brother-in-law to where her mother lived, so that I would know the way on my own in future. The following day her brother-in-law arrived from the Kasese district, and when I saw his bike I could not wait to go. As we raced through the vast hilly area covered by jungle I came to realise how far it would be on foot, but my fear was mixed with the excitement of riding the bike and holding on tight so I wouldn't fall off. The old woman, Jane, lived in a broken down hut covered with grass. There was only one room and their sleeping area looked like the stable.

She lived with her daughter and son, and I was surprised to hear them say they were happy with their life. I listened and observed their happiness in the middle of nowhere, living on the milk their few cows managed to provide. They had to walk four kilometres to a farmer to trade their milk for food, if they had enough. On our way home I looked carefully at the road, knowing I had to go back there alone soon. The only question my stepmother asked when we stopped was whether I had memorised the way.

A few weeks passed and I came home, leaving my bag at school because I was going back for evening classes.

After I had eaten my stepmother told me I had to take money to her mother, and I was terrified. When I thought about going alone through those dangerous hills I could barely see from fear and my tears of anger. Slowly I took a bag, packed one pair of underpants and a bottle of water. It was two o'clock in the afternoon when I left, and the burning African sun reminded me of the hell I was already in.

As I passed my school I looked at it, wishing I was there and my thoughts stayed there as I walked on. When I could no longer see the town I became even more afraid, and in the savannah I tried to walk as fast as I could. Even so, I stopped several times to listen for animals because I knew the area was full of monkeys and predators.

After I passed through the savannah, I noticed water coming out of the rocks. I checked my bottle and realised I had no water, so I went down to the stream and washed my head and face before I drank. I watched the small monkeys playing and having a good time. I looked at them, wishing I could be like them. When I looked down I saw gorillas standing in the middle of the road and a few in a tree. When they did not move I crept closer and watched. One of them was holding its baby and feeding. I saw the baby enjoy the love and care it received in its mother's arms.

I stood there afraid to move, until I spotted a small path that looked as though it had been made by animals.

I was afraid. It was the first time I had experienced such an event, and I was reminded of the story my sisters had told me. They had told me that big gorillas had small children. I was petrified and thought of going back the way I had come. But I thought of my stepmother and that if I went back, I would be grabbed and eaten.

I was confused, not knowing what I to do. I stood there for a long time. It was getting late and I started to cry, thinking I was going to die and leave my sisters behind. After waiting for a long time, I saw two men coming towards me. I decided to hide the money in my underwear.

"What are you doing here?" they asked. I told them my stepmother had sent me and finally the men made my day and took me to the old woman. I told her I was tired and wanted to sleep. She put an old blanket on the ground where we had to sleep. Even though I was tired I couldn't sleep because of the smell of old cheese that was everywhere.

The following morning the jungle was covered with moisture and the reds and yellows of the rising sun covered the morning sky. As I enjoyed the coolness behind the hut I saw a piece of paper that looked like money. I looked around to see if anyone was looking and realised I was alone. When I heard them calling me for the morning milk I hid the money in my underwear. I drank the milk with my heart in my throat, wondering whether I should give it back or not. The girl started looking for the note and then asked if I had seen it. With a smile I said no. But she kept on asking me, over and over again.

After I had said good-bye I walked slowly, trying not to let the money fall out of its hiding place. All along the way I thought about what I should buy. When I couldn't decide I let my stomach choose. Before I reached town I saw a small shop with a Pepsi Cola sign in its window where I bought two Mirandas, which I drank while the man stared at me. Then I told him to give me sweets for the rest of the money.

I continued on my journey and after about a kilometer I started to feel a pain in my stomach. I ignored the warning until I felt very thirsty. I sat down under some trees because I thought I was about to die. I found it difficult to get up. When I couldn't breathe I stuck my fingers down my throat and threw up.

The pain went away, but I felt hungry and tired. I managed to get up but felt a terrible dizziness, as though my head was spinning. I started walking once more handing out sweets to children I met on my way. When I got to my school I checked my desk, but my school bag was missing. I searched all over but it was nowhere to be found. I searched like a mad animal and tears of desperation ran down my face. I asked myself why such things had to happen to me. "What have I done to the world?" I asked myself. I tried feeling strong so I could go home, only my mind still managed to torture me.

I sat crying desperate tears in the middle of the playground, watching children getting ready to go home. Eventually I started making my way home, although I couldn't think clearly until later in the afternoon. Suddenly I remembered my friend, Rehema. I went to her uncle's home, thinking she would be able to help me. Before I got there I saw her from a distance and called her. "Rehema, you have to help me!"

She told me to wait down at the banana plantation until she could find a way of getting me into her room. I walked in the dark, hearing only my own footsteps. I sat down and looked around, afraid of what might grab me. I waited for a long time. I was so scared but she did finally appear, and together we made our way to her small room. She went into the house and came back with a plate of food. While we were eating her uncle called her and she told me not to eat until she came back. Rehema came back running, grabbed my hand and took me to the goat shed. She told me to sleep there because of the visitor who was going to sleep on Rehema's bed.

Early in the morning Rehema woke me up, and before leaving I told her how much I loved her. I walked through the plantation crying. I slept in the bushes for a few hours, but by midday I started feeling hungry, wishing I hadn't ever bought any Miranda.

I went close to the main road, sat there and began counting the cars, as I sang all the songs I knew, hoping to take away my sadness. When my stomach started rumbling, I lay down on my back, closed my eyes and began remembering my family and all the people who had ever been good to me. I tried to imagine how my real mother looked but my memory of her was too dim.

When I was about to be carried away by emotions, I stood up and began begging. I stood, holding out my arm, but no one seemed to notice me, until a man driving a brown car with "UCB" printed on its side, stopped. The man asked me why I was begging. I told him what had happened, so he gave me some money, telling me that if I waited for him, he would come back to help me.

As soon as he had left I went to Mr Monkey's stand and bought bananas and biscuits. I sat down and ate until I was full. I cleaned my hands in the grass and returned to the road to wait for the man. As I waited, I remembered telling the man my father's names and where he worked. I ran as fast as I could until I got to a place where I was sure that no one knew me or my father. I sat myself at the edge of the golf field. After long hours I realised that I was burning in the sun. I went from house to house asking for a job, but everywhere people asked me the same thing. How old am I? Who's your father? So I ended up running away from every house, and the day ended without finding any job. I thought of going back to Rehema but then I remembered the visitor. It was getting late when I saw the courthouse. Standing against the wall I began to sing quietly while I cried.

I woke with a fright the next day, and soon realised I was still safe. I walked down to the river and threw a few stones into the water. There was a cool breeze that refreshed me but I could smell the goats from the night before.

As I walked away from the water's edge I saw a house and decided to try once more to ask for work. I spent a long time standing outside looking at the door, listening to my pounding heart.

I ordered myself to knock on the door. I knocked and a man's voice said, "Coming!"

The door opened and a man looked at me with surprise. "What can I do for you?" He asked. With a smile he invited me inside to sit down and he asked me many questions.

I tried to answer his questions. The man told me that I could stay until his wife came home. I asked him what kind of work he had, and he told me that he was a doctor. "Why aren't you at work then?" I asked, but he looked troubled when he replied: "I have a problem with my legs. One of them is crippled, so I have to rest sometimes."

He explained that one leg was shorter than the other. "Which hospital do you work at?" I asked.

"Why?"

"Because I was wondering if you could do me a favour. If my stepmother and father come to your hospital, could you give them a big injection so they cry and scream like I always do?"

He looked straight at me and shook his head, not as a no to my request but as though he understood, a sad acknowledgement of my situation. After a quiet pause he asked me, "Do you love your father?" and I replied, "Yes, but he doesn't love me."

He asked me if I would cry if my father died, and I replied: "No, I would not cry if he died together with my stepmother, but I would if he died without her." He told me his job was to help people, not to harm them.

Then his wife came home and interrupted our conversation. She had a baby in her arms. "What if she is like my stepmother, and makes me take care of her baby too?" I thought, and I felt lost. The doctor's wife greeted me and I replied with a fright. She looked puzzled and asked what was troubling me. I replied, "Nothing, I was just looking at your baby."

She asked me if she should follow me back to my father's house. I didn't answer because I didn't know if she meant it as a question or as an order. I looked at her and asked if her husband had told her about my father. She said, "Yes."

"Are you not afraid of my father?" I asked. She just smiled, as though she didn't know what to answer. She gave me a nice bed in a cosy bedroom for the night. However, I wasn't very comforted because her words nagged at me, and I didn't know what morning would bring.

The following day, I was sitting on the sofa like a puppy, waiting for an answer from the kind doctor and his wife. She told me that they couldn't hire me because of my young age. "You have a family and we think you should go back home." She said I had to be strong and to take the beatings even if it was unfair because of the education I would receive. "Make yourself strong and let them do whatever they want," she said. "This is your life, and it is important that you go back home. You may not be able to understand why I can't help you now, but some day you will. I just don't want you some day to be alone, without any family."

I realised that I had no chance of staying. With many tears and a stuffed nose, I was still hoping she would let me stay. I wished I had something to pack so that I could delay my departure. Instead I washed my face and hands, only I was finished quickly, and I panicked. I searched for more to do but there were no more excuses for staying. She said goodbye. I opened the door and went into the street.

I stopped a little way from our house. Suddenly my stepsister and brother appeared. They seemed to have missed me. It didn't occur to me that they might love me. I thought they would only miss the work I did and the breakfasts I prepare for them. I wanted to know if my father was upset. They said they didn't think he was upset enough to beat me and there was no reason for me to be afraid of coming home, though I didn't believe them. It sounded like they had decided to per-suade me to come home. Then Ray suggested he go and ask his moth-er if I could return. He didn't take long and with the same dreadful suspicion as before, I decided to go back. I was a beggar with no choice – I had to take what was offered.

My stepmother questioned me about what had happened. She seemed calm and looked satisfied with my answers, and told me that she would try to soften my father when he returned. I felt relieved and trusted her because there was no mad shouting and yelling between us. Later that afternoon father returned from work, and I began preparing myself. I expected him to be happy to see me, but his rudeness stopped me from saying a word.

He just grabbed me and started to punch, without letting me explain anything. It went on and on. Then I noticed that my nose was bleeding and I found myself behind a locked door. So there I was, enveloped in darkness and bad memories.

One of my eyes was injured and I couldn't open it. I was afraid because I had promised myself always to protect them when I was beaten. I tore a peace of my clothes, soaked it with the blood from my nose, and started rubbing my eye as I hoped to open it. I felt a strong pain in one of my ribs and I was seriously afraid. I painted myself with blood to scare him away from beating me again. Then I started to kick the door, screaming and shouting. My father pulled me out of the room and stared at me with scared eyes before he said, "Oh my God!"

He told me to undress, took me to the bathroom, and with warm water he started washing the blood off my body. When I saw his sorry face, I felt secure enough to show him my ribcage, which revealed some bad marks. He told me he would take me to the hospital the following day. But he made it clear that if asked I must say I fell out of a tree. He promised that after we had been to the doctor he and I would go to town and buy me new clothes. I cried that night, not because of my body but because of my father's words. I could not remember any other time when my father had shown me affection, and it made everything seem so unreal. I also thought of my sisters and I cried until the sleep stole me away.

I woke up in a state of fright. My whole body was screaming with pain. I tried to get up but I could only crawl, and despite the terror of the pain I managed to get to my father. He told me to come nearer. He, reached out and touched my face. He then went away and returned with a doctor. The doctor never bothered to ask me what had happened because my father was standing right beside him. The doctor explained that because of the rib I needed to be taken to the hospital for further treatment.

My father looked at the doctor. He asked him what he should tell the hospital. The doctor said "There is only one way to do this and it will cost you money." "How much?" my father asked. "I am not sure," the doctor replied "but there is a friend of mine who may be able to help her." Another doctor came to see me and once more I had escaped death.

When I got better, my father kept his word and took me for the first time on a trip to town, and I felt very happy walking around with him. When we returned he gave me sweets, telling me to enjoy them. I was enjoying myself, but as soon as my father left my stepmother appeared like the lightning. She chased me out and told me not to return until I had finished my father's sweets. With those words I remembered what

Margie once said, that our stepmother's hatred for us would be with her until she died.

Rejected

WHENEVER ONE OF MY SISTERS CAME HOME, I saw that they carried their pain in different ways although they had the same memories as I did. I desperately wished they would take them with me when they left again. They tried to appear happy away from us, and my father believed them.

I saw this again when Helen came home with a new man. I had just returned from fetching water at a friend of my father's and was lying in front of our house, when I heard a car on the road. Then I saw Helen step out of a blue Suzuki. I hardly recognised her. She was very well dressed and had long hair. I was so excited that I tripped and fell as I ran to meet her. My father came out and stood at the door without saying a word. Before Helen could speak, my father wanted to know who the man in the car was. She told him this was the man she wished to marry. My father asked, "What language does he speak?"

"He comes from the east," she replied.

"So what is he doing here in the west?"

"I brought him here because I wanted you to meet him."

"Don't you understand that I can't approve of this marriage?" He replied.

"But he's very good to me, and if I marry him I will be happy. So what is your answer?" she asked.

My father snapped at her. "If you want to remain my daughter, don't marry him!"

My sister began to cry, and as if in heavy pain she slowly turned around and walked back to the car. All of a sudden, before opening the car door, she looked back and asked my father if he would just greet the man. "No!" my father roared. "And furthermore, you should know this, if you marry him, you must never come back again!" I watched my father crawl back to the house like a snake, as if nothing had happened.

Helen said goodbye to the man in the car, and I wondered what

words she said to this man that she almost married because they parted as though they had never known each other. Watching her cry, I saw
something in her eyes I couldn't understand and it made me sad. Then
I turned angrily and told her, "Our father is bad. You say this man
makes you happy, so why don't you leave and take me with you?" She
told me she was too scared to live without a father because of how a
man could treat her if he knew that she had nowhere else to go. I asked
what she would do now, and she told me that she had no idea. She was
not sure if she could still live with our stepmother's rules.

I was sad to hear this and begged her to stay for a little while, but
she couldn't stop crying. I became annoyed, so I went to Sofia's. At
night in my room I told Helen about Patricia, the woman who might be
able to help us find our mother. The next day Helen said goodbye with
a proud face, as if she would never return. I hoped with all my heart
that she would find our mother.

The rest of the day my father kept on complaining to himself, and
I remember him saying, "They always leave but come back to get my
help," and when he turned away, I looked at him and shook my head.
The following afternoon all of us sat on the veranda. Two men arrived
and told him he was wanted by the military police. When he asked
them what it was about they only said he would find out when they got
there.

"Why haven't you come with a car? Where are your uniforms?"
They answered, "Do not question us. Get up and you will know everything when you get there!"

My father looked afraid because in those days it was common for
people to be taken by mysterious men and to disappear without a trace.
I had heard about this, but I didn't care what happened to my father.
He told the men they could kill him right where he was standing
because he wasn't going anywhere. The men looked puzzled. Before
they left they told him they would return coming back with more soldiers. As soon as they had gone, my father ran through the banana
plantation. He came back with a group of soldiers.

The military men were northerners and they spoke a different language. We spoke Kinyankole. The soldiers stayed and the mysterious
men never returned. After this incident I tried to understand why this
had happened. When I saw my stepmother's face, it seemed to me that
she had something to do with it. But of course, my hatred for her could

have misled me. I thought about the strange soldiers, never dreaming that I too would wear that same uniform.

A week had passed since my sister left to search for our mother. I saw her return and thought of it as a memory, but when I looked again she was real. It was impossible for me to wait for her to come to me, so I ran towards her, and asked, "Did you find our mother?" Before she could answer I saw it in her eyes, and with sadness I knew that the journey had been a failure. She told me the woman I had sent her to was out of the country, and that she had waited together with Mutton and Judith but the woman never showed up.

My father shouted at us, "You leave me here, but you will always return because this is your home." His words made me realise that all he wanted was for his daughters to suffer while they were away and to punish them when they returned.

A few nice days passed, free of mad words, and a photographer came past. I asked my sister if we could take a photo of all of us since my photo had never been taken. I was very excited to see how I would look. As soon as the photographer left, my father came with sad words. He told Helen that a son of a friend of his wished to marry her.

During supper my sister told our father she would not marry the man. The look on his face showed me that the words only provoked his anger. Every evening my father would terrorise her with cruel words.

Helen had nowhere to live and had refused to marry the man my father had chosen for her. She was turned into a camel. She had to take care of everything. Every day when I came back from school I would help her. My stepmother was now reading novels and turned the garden into her private recreational centre.

When my father came home he would ask Helen for food. I wondered whether he had forgotten she wasn't his wife. Helen had been out to visit the neighbours, and when she returned my stepmother was furious as she had not cooked my father's supper. My father wanted to punish Helen but she went wild as though she had been stung by bees. She asked him what kind of father he was, torturing and beating his own children. The wrath was all over his face, and he seemed to grow to a terrible size. Helen shouted at him, "You are not going to beat me ever again! " He told her to get out but Helen refused saying "I am going nowhere and if you want to kill me, do it now!" My father tried to drag her out of the house but she was strong enough to resist him.

She refused to live by our stepmother's rules.

Later she called me to follow her outside, gave me a letter for our father, and left. This is what the letter said:

John,

You made me live my childhood so differently from other children. I am now wandering around in the world without purpose. You have failed to choose between your child and your wife. You have not shown me love but still you claim that I am your blood. You have buried me in deep thoughts. I am going now and I will die in pain though I will never call out for you. You will die with guilt and never ask yourself why. I hope that you will feel the same pain that you have caused me.

Helen

After I read the letter, I wondered whether I should give it to my father or not. I tore it into small pieces, afraid of what would happen to me if I gave it to him. The sister I had called a traitor now became my hero. I remembered her words because she stood up for what she believed in. She suffered a great deal in her short life but never asked for help until the day she returned to die at home.

Murderous Lie

I WAS ALONE AGAIN ONCE HELEN HAD LEFT, and the happiness I had gained was taken away from me as suddenly as it had come. I was sad not knowing where my sister had gone. I found it hard to find where to start and where to end, as I thought of following in her foot-steps. My eyes refused to help me sort good from bad solutions, and as the days went by the pain grew stronger.

One morning the milkman didn't arrive, so I had to go and fetch the milk from the dairy. My father gave me money to get the milk. Right there in front of the bank I saw soldiers, and as I came closer they start-ed staring at me. They scared me and I panicked. I walked past them as fast as I could. At the dairy I found I had lost the money, so I went back again thinking that I might get lucky and find it. I searched all over but it wasn't anywhere. I was thinking of what my father had done to my sisters when they had lost money, however I calmed myself down thinking he probably would not punish me as badly because I was so young.

When I reached home he had already gone to work, and my step-mother left my story for my father to solve. That day I missed school, and whenever I looked at the watch my heart would jump, wishing a car would hit my father so he would never return. In the evening he returned, and I heard him talk with my stepmother. Too little time passed and he called me and shouted, "You bastard! How could you lose the money?"

I told him what had happened, knowing perfectly well that he too was afraid of the soldiers. But my father was not convinced and told me that he was keeping me out of school. I felt cold all over as I looked him in the eyes. Then I went to bed. I lay in my bed staring at the ceiling and wanting to cry, but my eyes were dry.

Days later our father arrived with a truck and some people to whom he used to sell cows. He stayed behind letting the driver finish the deal in town. The next day my brother, Richard, returned from grazing the cows and told me that a cow had hidden its newborn calf somewhere in the thick bush. We wondered whether we should tell our grandmother or our father. We agreed on telling Grandmother so my brother could prepare himself. I watched from a distance when he told her and almost immediately I heard a scream coming from the house.

I ran to see what had happened and saw grandmother on her way to our father, who was on the other side of the house repairing the fence. My father marched inside the house found a chair and sat down, with his face lowered. A few seconds later he jumped up, glaring at my brother as though he had flames in his eyes. I saw my brother move towards the door and stand next to it. My father said that at that moment the calf was probably being eaten, and then he went back to his chair.

We spent a moment just sitting, and I breathed a sigh of relief, thinking that everything was over. "Bastard! You've given my calf to the lions!" My father suddenly roared through the silence, as he reached for his *machete*. My brother disappeared out of the door as fast as the wind.

My father followed with his machete raised and charged after him like a madman. I was left behind, thinking that my brother would be killed. I kept looking at my grandmother, thinking she might do something. She merely looked back at me with angry eyes.

I went quietly to bed and waited there, as I feared what the outcome would be. Some time later my father returned, ordered me out of bed, and then showed me the machete covered in blood, telling me that he had killed my brother. His words made me strong because I knew that I had nothing to gain or lose. I didn't cry or shake anymore, I just felt the world get a little colder. I went to bed with dry eyes, remembering my brother and the good times we had had together, hoping all the cows would die. I was hurt to see that my brother had to die because of the cows. But then I thought of the love that made the cow hide its child, and that stopped my wish. I realised that the animal's love for her young was ten times as pure as anything I had seen in people.

I got up earlier than anyone else and went to search for my brother's body. After a short walk I saw the figure of a young boy standing on top of a termite hill. I walked towards him, hoping he had seen my brother's body. As I got closer I discovered that it was my brother, and before I could say a word, he spun around, took his pants off and showed me his bum. I almost laughed my head off and when he came down the hill I gave him a big hug and told him what had happened after the chase.

The only thing that mattered was that he was still alive. I told him to stay there, so that I could go and steal some food. When I reached home my father had gone to the workers' house, and I managed to steal food and milk and return without our grandmother noticing. Later my father returned and I remembered to keep my face sad until he returned to the town house.

The Whisper

IT WAS HARD FOR ME TO SEE THAT there had been any good times with my stepmother. I cannot think of any happiness I might have shared with her. She seemed to strike whenever things started to go right.

It was Saturday morning after the cows had been counted, and it seemed that fifteen were missing. Two workers quickly ran to Grandmother. I saw her hair rise off her head and with anger she asked where Mike was. Just as they were about to start searching, Mike arrived and it seemed as if he had been out jogging. He asked why everyone was assembled like that. My grandmother told him he shouldn't act as if he didn't know what he had done. But Mike seemed unaware of what Grandmother meant, until she told him he had helped thieves to steal the cows. Mike swore to his innocence. He asked her why, if he had stolen the cows, would he come back to be caught?

But she was not convinced. After intimidating Mike she sent one of the workers to call my father. My brother and I told Mike to run away but he refused, saying he was a Tutsi and our father would understand that he had not stolen his cows.

In the afternoon my father and the police arrived, and Mike's words became meaningless. The police decided to listen to my father who was talking as though his feet were on fire. Mike was beaten and kicked by the police before being dragged into their Landrover. In the evening, just before we went to bed, my father told my brother and I to stop looking after the cows because thieves might attack us. But I didn't listen much because I could still see the police beating Mike.

Early in the morning my father and one of the workers went to search for the cows and I hoped so much that the thieves would kill my father, but he returned empty- handed a few days later. But there was still one more thing for him to worry about. Mike had been set free, and the only thing I could see in my father's eyes was revenge. He began a random search and bribed neighbouring ranch workers to help him find Mike.

Very early in the morning a man came to tell my father that Mike had been offered a job. Father quickly ran into the house, grabbed a rope and left with one of the workers. In the afternoon, my brother and I returned from the dam and found Mike lying near the house. We could barely recognise him. His clothes were covered in blood, and he was near the house, with his arms tied firmly behind his back, still surrounded by my father and his men. When Mike saw us he tried to raise his head, saying he was thirsty. My brother went inside and returned with a cup of milk, but father took the cup and threw the milk in Mike's face. "If you hadn't stolen my cows, none of this would have happened!" He shouted at him. Then my father grabbed an iron pipe and hit him on the back until he vomited blood. Mike's screams frightened me. I ran into the house and hid.

When everything was quiet I came outside again. Mike couldn't move, and when I saw my father's eyes I saw fear crawl across his face. He looked away and ordered the workers to put Mike on the wheelbarrow and dump him in the bush.

The following morning father brought the police. He told them Mike had been caught stealing cows again, and when the workers beat him he died. When I heard his terrible lie I looked at him with fiery hatred. I wished that my look would burn him!

My father went inside the house. I quickly told an officer the real story and begged him not to tell my father. When my father returned from the house they handcuffed him, while telling him that they did not believe his story. Grandmother cried aloud when they took her son. I just smiled.

I called my brother and told him that now we were free.

A Light in the Darkness

A WEEK PASSED. With no father and no stepmother we had a good time. Grandmother was quiet and didn't pay much attention to us. One day, on our way back from hunting we saw Margie.

She believed my father would be in prison for a long time for such a serious crime. Then she asked whether our stepmother's children had been removed from school too. When we said no, I nearly ran away from fear – she was very angry when she heard my reply.

With a face like a snake about to strike, she ordered us to get ready to go back to school. A few days later, she forced our stepmother to allow my brother and I to return to school.

Then I heard Margie say she was going to see my father. I wanted to see how he felt in prison. As we got closer, the prison warders stared at us. One of them called my sister and when she went up to him I was afraid, thinking that they might harm her or throw her in prison. I was impressed to see my sister face them without fear. She smiled and her pretty face made the man let us through the gate. A few minutes later a man brought my father to us. He was wearing grey shorts and a short-sleeved shirt, and I was surprised to see him looking bald.

We went to an empty room together. The man in charge commanded him to sit on the concrete floor. My father looked embarrassed and could only sit staring at the floor. He spoke only to Margie. All I saw on his face was a forced smile.

My father and Margie got into an argument over us not being in school. I felt sorry for my father and silently I pinched my sister, trying to make her stop the argument. But she continued until my father was ordered back to his cell without time to say goodbye.

At home Margie got ready to return to Kampala. When she had gone, my stepmother moved me to a cheaper school, and Richard was sent back to the farm.

The new school was more exciting for me. The teachers seemed to understand me better, and I was appointed class monitor. But when it came to being with other children I felt too insecure. I couldn't tell them who I was, not because I felt inferior, but because I knew most people disliked Tutsis. The children made fun of me because I looked different, and I couldn't find a way to explain why. I lied and pretended I belonged to the same people as they did. But my face, my small lips and pale skin marked me as different. Later I learned that no matter how many lies I told, they never helped me to change into their kind.

Time passed. Margie had been gone for a while and my stepmother sold a cow every week. Her reason for this was she needed to free our father from debt and that she needed to pay our school fees. It annoyed me to see her sisters come and go. I was jealous because she was giving away my father's money. While my father was away, her mother, Jane, arrived with one of her daughters. Jane left her at our farm which made me desperate and confused. My stepmother never visited my father. I thought he would never return and that my stepmother would steal all his riches and then chase me away.

At school things were tough for me. Previously I had been known as the one with an answer to every question. Now I couldn't concentrate on anything. At the end of class my teacher would ask why I was like that but I had no answer – I just didn't think she would take me seriously. One afternoon I returned home and Margie was there. I had returned from Sofia's just in time to hear Margie threaten our stepmother with beatings if she didn't stop selling the cows. She had been selling one cow every week! She said she needed the money to get my father released and to pay for our school fees. Margie started to pay money to the police and within a few weeks my father was released.

After Margie left, my major concern was whether father would take me out of school or not. He spent some time not working and being a good father. But then he began to drink. He would return at night, waking everyone with his crashing through the house to his bed. One night he woke all of us. He called us all to the living room and told each one of us what he wanted us to do with our lives.

One day I heard him accuse my stepmother of sleeping with a boy who was living at our neighbour. I heard my father say, "I can even smell sperm all over the house." Then he dragged her out of the door and fought with her in the garden. A week later my father got his old job back and he stopped drinking. My stepmother however soon got up to her old tricks, and this time she demanded that I prepare dinner because she was going to Mrs Derrick.

I tried to imagine how the sauce looked when she made it. It was yellowish and tasty, but that was all I knew. I decided to put in half a litre of fish oil and a lot of curry, but I was afraid of the salt. When I had finished I felt satisfied – it looked similar to my stepmother's and I knew that she would thank me for it. When she returned she went straight to the kitchen, looked at the food and went back to the living room without a word.

I stood at the door still waiting for her to thank me but she didn't say a thing. I kept wondering what she saw in my food. I was as proud as any other little girl about what I had made, so I was sure she saved her thanks for everyone to hear during supper. When my father came home she gave me the food to bring to the table. We all sat down and were about to eat when my father shouted, "Woman! Is this the food you have cooked for me?" And my stepmother replied, "Ask your daughter..."

"Why should I ask my daughter when you are my wife?" father replied. She told him that she had come home from a friend and found that I had cooked the food without being told. My father looked at me like a dog about to bite, and asked me who told me to cook. I just looked down without replying. He told Ray to fetch a bunch of chillies from the garden which he mixed into his soup. Then he ordered me to eat it.

I knew that even if I had the food he would still beat me, so it didn't matter what I did. He repeated his order until he gave up. Then he walked to his room and came back with a stick. He stood in front of me and ordered me to lie down. I remained seated. He sat himself on a chair and held my head in a tight grip between his legs. I decided to fight, trying to make him break the fuelled lamp which was hanging from the ceiling, hoping that the splintering glass would kill us all.

My father began beating me all over. I tried to protect my back with my arms but a sharp pain in my fingers made me give up the fight. Then I heard my stepbrothers and sisters pleading and crying: "Please father, stop, you're killing her!" They told the children to go to bed and left, leaving me to help myself. After a while Ray and Pamela came back and helped me to wash away the blood. They helped me into bed, and it warmed me when Pamela asked me if she could sleep next to me. I had a talk with her about our parents, and she told me that she hated our parents for what they had done.

In the morning my father said I should say that I fell from a tree if anyone asked what had happened, otherwise he would beat me again. I walked to school very slowly, and when I arrived all the children gathered around me asking what had happened, but my tears just ran down my face. Because I said nothing the children fetched a teacher. She began asking too, so I told my father's lie but she didn't believe me, and took me to the principal's office. He assured me that anything I said would remain between him and me, but I stayed silent, staring at the floor. Then he asked me if the woman at home was my real mother. "Yes," I replied. But he kept on pressuring me for a different answer, and after a struggle I confessed. He took a pen and began writing with a determined face and a steady hand. When he had finished he told me to give it to my father, assuring me that it was nothing to worry about.

At home I gave it to my father, and after having read it he roared. I waited outside for some time. I was very worried until my father came to tell me to deliver the letter he held in his hand. After the morning parade I gave the principal my father's letter and waited for him to read it. He looked up shaking his head and looked down at me, before taking me to his office. He then told me that the letter he had written the day before was an attempt to persuade my father to let him coach and take care of me at his home.

On my way home, I went through our neighbour's field of sweet potatoes, sat down and looked at my fingers. I dug up a potato with my other hand and started chewing it, thinking very hard. I thought about my sisters. "Can I rely on them? Do they remember me, or are they busy struggling for themselves?" I stood up, looked at our house from a distance, and discovered I was gaining strength. This was the time to stand up for myself, before my stepmother destroyed my soul.

Stranger in a Strange Land

AS MY FINGERS STARTED TO HEAL my stepmother seemed uneasy, as if things weren't going the right way, and I saw her behaviour as a warning of stormy weather. My father remained peaceful and I could only guess he was waiting for my injuries to heal. School was going to close for the holidays – I wasn't pleased because I hated being at home. Early in the morning, I ironed my uniform and ran to school. I found everyone already gathered in the assembly hall. Later I learned I was one of the few children without a parent there. I watched the prizes being prepared, thrilled with excitement as I hoped to be number one. The principal walked up to the podium with papers and began thanking us, the class monitors and the prefects. Then the moment came when he read out the prize-winners' names according to their position. My ears were wide open, expecting to hear my name first. Two other names were read before mine, but I didn't cry much because I got a prize anyway. When I opened it I found beautiful colours, rulers and a set of twelve learning books with funny pictures.

When our principal set us free we knew the war was at hand. We ran as fast as we could to get our sticks. We did this every year to get one last chance to fight with the children we didn't like. We got ourselves into small gangs and we'd attack and then run away. But we knew that it would all be forgotten by the new year.

After the battle, my friends and I headed for home, chatting and comparing injuries before we parted. I was almost home when my best friend, Sofia, came running, and before I could ask what was wrong, she told me not to go home. She told me that my stepmother had been watching me. Sofia had heard her say she would tell my father to beat me again for not hurrying home.

I struggled to hold back my tears before telling her that I would go and try to find my mother. I thanked her and told her not to say anything when she got home. I walked away and looked behind me. Sofia was still standing there. Then my tears broke out and I cried all the way to Patricia. She was standing outside with her son and two daughters, very surprised to see me.

"Does your father know you are here?" I said no. Patricia shook her head when I showed her my broken fingers, but asked me what help I wanted. "Just take me to my mother," I answered. She looked down and said that she couldn't help me because she was afraid of my father, so I threatened her, saying I would drink poison if she forced me to go back. As we sat there in her garden, we saw Pamela and Ray standing in the road. Quickly Patricia told me to run into the house, but I was sure they had spotted me.

She invited me inside with a nervous gesture, as if she were afraid they might return. Judith and Mutton invited me to their bedroom. They had lots of funny and beautiful toys I had never seen, making me forget all my troubles. We had dinner, and afterwards she showed me a photo of my mother and told me I looked like her. She told me a few things to help me with my journey, and I was relieved to know my mother lived at the end of the route.

It was 1984, and early in the morning, Patricia took me to the bus, bought me a ticket and we parted. I was crying silent tears, thinking of what I had started. As we were half way, the bus stopped all of a sudden at an alien place, and to my horror I saw an army roadblock. Everybody was ordered to stand in a line in front of the bus. They began searching the grown-ups and their belongings. They even beat some of the passengers with their guns. Those who had no identification were accused of being rebels and were taken into the bush by two soldiers.

We were told that the bus wasn't going any further because of rebel forces who might hijack the bus. The conductor began refunding people for their tickets, but I had lost mine. I begged him to give me my money – he refused. The man who had been sitting next to me asked why I was crying, so I told him that I was going to my mother. He asked me if I knew where she was and I answered yes, fearing that he would take me back to my father. I was relieved when he asked me to join him.

We all started walking, and the strange man asked my mother's names. But he already knew who she was because of her husband who was the chief of the town hall. He was a rich man with influence. When he said this I got angry, and asked myself why she hadn't used her husband's power to rescue us. We walked for many hours until we at last reached a building. My friend went to a restaurant, leaving me outside. I sat there looking at the people eating and drinking, but it didn't take away my need, so I walked around. I saw the police station and the buildings adjacent to it, which reminded me of the description Patricia had given me. I asked some women standing outside the police station if they knew my mother. No one did, so I walked back to be sure the man didn't leave me behind.

I started to doubt whether the man was my friend, seeing him eating without me through the window. Soon people from the bus had gathered outside the restaurant and our journey continued through the bush. It seemed we had entered a neverending wasteland, with bushes and trees scattered across a huge plain stretching to the horizon. The animals were full of life and made me believe I was the only miserable creature in the world. As I walked, my mind darkened, and I felt that neither good nor bad mattered anymore.

Though I was used to walking long distances, this walk made my legs burn. At one point I realised that no matter what I did, I could not keep up with them so I found my own pace and lagged behind. I fell down, tired and sad. "Get up!" I heard the strange man command, as he helped me to my feet. I told him to leave me there. I didn't want to go any further. A burning slap on my cheek made me stand up, and roused me enough for me to carry on walking.

The next thing I knew we had arrived at a house. It was already dark, and before he left he told me I had to sleep there until the following day. The old man living there seemed to be in the big house by himself, although I didn't know for sure because he didn't say much. Still, his silence made me feel comfortable.

He served supper and we ate without saying a word. Then he showed me where to bathe myself before showing me to bed. I was so exhausted that not even my frustration could keep me awake. In the morning I felt stronger and got a closer look at the old man. He was short, shabbily dressed and bald on the top of his head, but around his ears and the top of his neck the hair was white. During breakfast there was a knock on the door, and the strange man from the day before picked me up. Before leaving, I thanked the old man and thought of his kindness as I walked through his green garden that led to the main road.

When I thought about the woman I was going to call my real mother, I became afraid. The only mother I knew was mean and cunning. It was hard for me to imagine any woman would be able to love me.

But there was no turning back. Besides, I had no choice. Now I was a beggar prepared to take all kinds of chances. After walking for some time we came across two women on the road, and the man pointed at one of them, telling me that she was my mother. When she approached us I almost ran away. He told the woman that I was looking for her, and I froze as she began staring at me. I couldn't recognise her from the photos I had seen at Patricia's. This woman looked a lot older.

She asked me my names as well as my father's and sister's. When I replied, her eyes opened wider and my fear rose when the man said goodbye. I wondered whether to follow the man or not, when the woman smiled and took my hand. I could see she wasn't sure, and it became worse when she didn't know which one of her daughters I was. She looked happy to see me, so I just had to walk at her side. She started to annoy me by telling me the terrible things my father had done to her.

We approached a huge house, surrounded by a beautiful garden with many trees and flowers. Even before we entered her house she shouted for the workers to slaughter a cow. She left me in front of the house and I ran back the way we had come. I rounded the house to see if her husband was home, but when I found no sign of him, I entered the house. I walked quickly from room to room. In one of the bedrooms there was some money on the table. I looked at it and was about to walk away but I took a few steps back and took some of it.

I acted this way because I sensed that something might happen, and I knew that with money I could find another way. After a while she returned with men and women and soon all the women were grabbing pots and knives. The men rushed to prepare the fire, while my mother ran around speaking so fast I could only understand when I heard my name.

Evening came and we sat around the table. Others sat in the garden eating. Everywhere I looked I saw the same convincing smile and my heart was full of fear because I couldn't tell if they were happy to see me or happy to eat me. I knew that somewhere people had small children. I looked at all the food that was on the table, and I hoped that everybody would be satisfied.

The big feast came to an end and the guests left. I was alone with the woman who was supposed to be my mother. She put me to bed, said good-night to me and went to her own bedroom. Lying in bed I couldn't help thinking about this family and their visitors. I was afraid they might return to eat me, so I listened very carefully to every sound in the house. I listened for knives being sharpened or footsteps in the garden. When I couldn't hear anything anymore, I got up. Being very careful not to make a sound, I got dressed. I walked through the house like a cat, and crept outside into the night.

My heart was too cold and my suspicion had no end. My mother's love and care could not find its way into my heart.

Part Three

A New Family

A Mark for Life

I STOOD ON THE MAIN ROAD, deciding whether to go back to the old man. I would tell him what had happened. Maybe he would let me stay and work for him.

I felt scared standing out there with the moon and stars with their bright light shining brighter than any street light. I walked and walked, and after some time I noticed something was wrong. I hadn't seen the old man's house and wondered whether it was the same way I had come the day before.

I couldn't feel my body. I stood there trying to think and when I couldn't find a solution I got on a train. I woke up when the train stopped and it was still night outside.

I got off the train and walked until I saw the end of the road. All my fear had gone and I felt stronger than ever. Then I saw a flash of light and thought of turning back. I was exhausted. I decided to walk towards the light but was stopped by a man's voice. "Stop! Who are you? Come closer," he ordered. He was surprised when he looked down at me.

"What are you doing out here in the middle of the night?" He asked. "I'm looking for my mother," I replied. He pointed his torch at me and asked about my father. "He's dead," I lied. I was still answering questions when a group of men appeared from the bush with guns on their shoulders. Everybody stood there looking at me and I was very afraid.

I relaxed when some of the men began to speak my language. All of them were very dirty, and they were dressed in torn clothes. The man seemed content with my answers and told me to go to sleep. I was puzzled and kept on looking at him, wondering where the house and bed was. Suddenly he smiled and laid two torn blankets on the ground. He told me to sleep. Although the blanket smelled bad, mosquitoes forced me to cover my head with it. I woke up to the voice of a man commanding, "Left–right, left–right," and when I looked around, I saw children of different ages marching next to a man in military uniform. I could feel an excitement growing in my stomach. It was like a brand new game and I wished that I was there marching along with them.

The man from yesterday approached me with friendly, but strange eyes. Before he could speak I asked to join the others, but he refused because of my swollen feet. Soon after getting up we all had to leave. I couldn't understand why. Some of the children knew why. They said that the NRA had just attacked Kabamba military barracks, and we had to move to a new place.

The NRA had many groups and each one had its own operational areas. We never stayed in one place. We were always on the run from the government army. We moved our camp to another place, and on the third day I was allowed to join, and I felt excited as I marched alongside with them.

After what might have been two hours of marching we had a break of fifteen minutes. The grown-ups sat alone and the children sat in groups. I sat alone looking at their faces, and many of the children seemed to have been there for some time. It was hard for me to join in with them because I didn't speak their language. After the break, some were lined up behind gun lines at a practice site. There were twelve children, each with an AK47. They had a few seconds to dismantle their guns and to put them back together again.

The following day we trained in taking cover and charging with bayonets, but the AK47s were bigger than most of us so we charged with wooden sticks. On the third day of my training an instructor came straight towards me in the line at the morning parade. The hard-looking tall man stood in front of me, looking straight down into my eyes, and asked my name. Scared and frightened, I looked down. "Look at me, China eyes!" He roared and my head shot up to meet his eyes. Then he pulled me out of the line and commanded me to march in front of the others: "China! Left-right, China, left-right!" From that day on I was known as "China".

My foreign name made me famous, and most of the children became my friends, although our different languages were a problem. I spoke Kinyankole and there were only a few who spoke it. I had to learn Kiganda and Swahili as fast as I could. Most of the kids were of the Baganda tribe who speak Kiganda, but Yoweri Museveni considered Swahili as the language we ought to speak, as it belonged to no one. He thought using an 'international' language would end tribalism. He taught us that the differences between us shouldn't matter any more because we were all fighting for freedom.

My training didn't take very long – not because I was a fine child soldier who would be fearless on the battlefield, and not because I was a fast learner. The simple reason was the NRA was short of men, and they could not afford to spend time training new soldiers.

After being taught a little about warfare, we were divided into different fighting groups. I was one of those who couldn't carry an AK47, so we helped carry the leaders' things – cups, pans, ammunition.

A month had passed since I'd left the training grounds. I was then picked for a special assignment along with a few other children. I was excited because I would be seeing the action I had heard so much about from the older children. We walked through the bush, getting our instructions along the way. Soon we hid on the perimeter of the bush that surrounded the dirt road. The commander told us to go to the middle of the road, sit down and pretend to have a good time playing with the sand. After a while, government troops approached in a huge convoy, but we continued playing as though we were alone. The convoy stopped – the first cargo truck was right in front of us. When most of the soldiers jumped out, we did as we had been instructed, running back into the bush to our fighting group, who then opened fire on the enemy. But it didn't happen quite as I had been told. The sound was terrifyingly loud and everything on the road seemed to splinter into pieces as rocket-propelled grenades (RPGs) hit the trucks.

I was more frightened than ever, and about to run for my life when one of my comrades held me down behind a tree.

Our side won, and after the battle everybody ran to the road and began undressing the dead soldiers. Every one of us, except the senior officers, needed something to wear. It didn't matter that it was the enemy's military uniform – anything was okay with us. I stood and watched from a distance as the enemy's boots and underwear were shared out. I was confused, having been told that I was fighting for freedom. I never imagined that it would include stealing from the dead.

My excitement turned into sadness when I saw the wounded enemy scattered around crying for help, and suddenly it became hard for me to think of them as my enemy. Those who had surrendered had their arms tied behind their backs in the most painful way. When I looked around at my comrades they seemed to be enjoying themselves. It convinced me there was nothing on earth the human beings liked more than to torture and laugh at their prey. The captured troops were escorted to our camp. Our comrades kicked them and spat at them, and when we arrived, the officers were shot dead. Yoweri Museveni welcomed us with convincing words. For playing with the sand we became the heroes of the day.

We had supper with the big man himself, outside his little African hut, where each of was given a uniform and a pair of boots that belonged to the officers. That night we were allowed a good night's rest, while the grown ups guarded the camp. Our camp had only three huts.

The following morning we had to look for a new camp because we feared the government would send in helicopters and artillery in retaliation for the ambush of the day before. Getting around in our new clothes required a lot of skill. The boots went far above our knees, and the uniforms almost swallowed us, making it difficult for us to walk through the bush. But there was a woman who walked with us who made it a little easier. At one point all of us children were crying from hunger and thirst. Museveni ordered the troops to set up camp and cook dried beans and corn. Some collected firewood and others searched for water. Museveni sat in the shade under a tree with two women, both called Narongo, and some of the officers.

Among the officers was a girl nicknamed "Mukombozi", the Liberator. Mukombozi was rescued by the NRA when government troops killed her family. She was on the jeep when the NRA shot at it with an RPG.

The soldiers died but she survived but she had forgotten her name forever. She was known to be a brave and dedicated girl who refused to carry anything except the weapon that had saved her. Mukombozi and one of the two Narongos were best friends. One night, at the campfire, Narongo told us the story of why she was with the NRA. One day, government soldiers had broken into her family home looking for NRA rebels. They beat and tortured her husband, and then shot him with his hands tied behind his back. Then they shot her twins right in front of her. Like many orphans in NRA, Narongo was a Mugandan, who'd been born in the Ruwero district. She was loving towards the children in the NRA, and none of us will ever forget her.

With tears in her eyes, she promised to get revenge on those responsible for the death of her family. She took her AK47 as her husband – it was always by her side, waiting for the day of revenge when the NRA would be in power.

The Battle

MY GROUP AND I WERE AT A PLACE near Rwenzori, resting away from the sun. It was around three o'clock in the afternoon when Salem Saleh, a senior officer and Museveni's younger brother, arrived. In his briefing he told us it was time for the NRA to overthrow Dr Milton Obote. I saw him smile as he said it. He and the mobile brigade had captured something called a Katusha, a special weapon, the day before. This had struck a blow to Obote's soldiers.

Before leaving us he assured us the NRA would be in power within weeks. Our morale was strengthened by his assurance and left us singing. Soon after Saleh left, our battalion commander took over the briefing. He told us to prepare ourselves because we were to attack a government camp about four kilometres away. After the briefing my friends and I just looked at each other, saying nothing. I prepared my Uzi, and then stripped off the side pockets and shortened my huge uniform. When I put it on again I felt lighter and safer because I knew that the amount of ammunition I carried would decide whether I survived or not. I was afraid but couldn't show it, as I was scared I would be called a coward – we were always checking one another to see who was afraid. If you were afraid, many of the children would laugh at you and we all hated that.

Many of us would do anything to be seen as heroes, and it didn't matter that we were scared – we still pretended to be cool. A woman soldier told us to sleep and slowly we made our beds on the grass. It was a struggle because the mosquitoes and my anxiety would not let me sleep. All night I wondered what I ought to feel. Staring at the starlit sky, I tried to feel the right way until the time came to shed blood.

Guided by the moon and the stars, we walked through the bush until we found our fellow soldiers already in position. Our platoon commander told us to kneel down and wait for our orders. Still safely hidden in the shadow of the last trees, we looked at the sleeping enemy camp. We waited for half an hour with the painful stings of busy mosquitoes draining our blood. We couldn't defend ourselves because we'd been told not to make a sound. All I did was bite my lips. Then we heard the first rapid fire of AK47s, which meant that now we had to kill every living thing in the camp.

Men and women began running out of the camp, some of them dropping down in one big mess, still naked. I saw them with their clothes still in their hands.

The massive fire of our guns made the wild screaming of goats, hens and people get fainter and fainter over the next three or four hours. When we entered the camp, goats and hens were lying in a heap with soldiers and their women who had been visiting. They were all dead, baking there in the hot morning sun.

We collected all the weapons and food we could carry and tied the arms of our captured enemy at the elbows. When we got back to our camp, the prisoners were ordered to dig their own graves and some of our officers told us to spit in their eyes. The enemy was told that no bullets would be wasted on them. I could feel tears dropping in my heart while I watched the enemy being told how they were to be killed.

"After you have dug your graves, I will call for the best men who will hit you on your head with an *akakumbi* – a short but heavy hoe. After the men had finished digging they were ordered to stand next to their graves. They were hit on their foreheads and on the back of their heads until they dropped into the graves and died. When it was over we had to move on because the enemy who was better equipped than we were didn't leave us alone for long. Sometimes we had to walk for a whole day without camping anywhere because military helicopters would pass over our heads, telling us to give up or face what they called "wipe-out". But we couldn't give up because we had already promised, we had crossed our hearts saying we would finish what we'd started. We walked with our belongings on our heads, trying to keep up with the grown-ups in a place burning like fire, with our small dry lips crying for water.

Just as I lost all hope they decided to end our pain and one of the commanders suggested we go to a nearby village to ask for water. We were never particularly careful when approaching a village because most of them supported the NRA. There was usually just scouting around, always with a slow moving head and eyes trying to see all around you, as far as possible.

As we approached the village, we were alarmed by the smell of rotten meat, but we ignored it and carried on. In the village we saw our fellow comrades lying on the ground with liquid leaking out of every opening they had in their body. I shook my head and closed my eyes. I realised there was much destruction still to come. I knew I couldn't change my situation. I tried as hard as I could to look after myself because I knew that hardly anybody managed to escape and no one could see their families. The ones who tried to get away were captured and suffered terrible deaths – we had seen it happen right in front of us. And even those who stole food from civilians were tied to trees and shot.

Civilians were always good to us – they gave us some of their cows and other food, but it was never enough for us.

After going through the village, a government helicopter suddenly appeared. We had to quickly throw ourselves down and hide. We waited for the heavens to fall on us.

After the terror had ended and we felt safe enough we stood up in panic, feeling our bodies to see if we were hit. After checking myself I looked around to see if any of my friends were hurt, and to my despair one of them was lying on the ground. When I walked towards him he was quiet, as though in a heavy sleep. I tried to wake him up but he didn't respond. It was hard for me to believe that he was going away from us. He was a small wise child who always comforted us, telling us to be strong and not to worry.

A minute or two passed and our platoon sergeant took us away from him, telling us he was dead. We had no time to cry. We joined the group and continued walking. My thirst and hunger were replaced with silent tears and I saw flashes of our comrades dead on the ground in the village. I was confused and afraid because I finally realised the terror I had seen could also happen to me.

Finally we arrived at a place with water. Beside it was a bush where we were told to rest.

I was woken by Museveni who arrived with a group of soldiers. He stood there in front us, as always with a stick in his hands. He was wearing a plain Franklin army jacket. He told us to sit closer to one another so that we could hear every word he was going to say. I was seated in front, and I looked Museveni straight in the eyes, but he kept on looking away, pretending that he did not notice me. I felt bad, because I thought that he had forgotten me. In his speech, he told us that we were fighting for freedom and against *ukabira* or tribalism. He said that the most important for us NRA fighters was to fight with one spirit so we could save those who were in government jails for crimes they had never committed.

As most children didn't know what had happened to their parents, he told us that they were killed by government troops and those who were still alive were in jails, and their hope was for us to liberate them. Everybody stood and shouted: "Yes, Mzee, yes Afande!" with our guns in the air. Museveni smiled and held his stick in the air as well. But I was different. I knew where my parents were. I just hoped to stay alive so that one day I could go home and kill them. I decided they had to pay the price for the pain I was in.

When Museveni finally left we began cooking the dried beans and corn. They took an eternity to cook. We children were standing against the trees, while others were scattered around in the grass. We had red eyes because we hadn't had any sleep for days. Everyone was quiet, except for a few low remarks now and then. We just stood there with our eyes on the pots waiting for the food.

Suddenly we heard a scream of warning and looked up in alarm. There was our OP (look-out man), running towards us with a wild face. He shouted so we could all hear that the enemy were a small distance away from us. Some of us put our hands in the hot water to save some of the food because we knew that this was probably the last meal for days.

We ran as fast as we could between the trees and grass, away from the enemy. When we reached what we believed was a safe place, we discovered some of us were missing. I suppose that because of their hunger they couldn't keep up with the rest of us.

There were many comrades that found it difficult to believe that we, the NRA, could win the war. Many soldiers gave up on life because of the intolerable conditions under which we lived. They gave up and stopped hoping for the day when we would take over and they would be offered a promising new life. They saw many of their comrades die, knowing it could be them the day after. For us it was different. The memories of our past lives and our awareness of death were limited. We fought with one spirit, totally committed to our cause.

The soldiers, however, would always take cover and dodge the bullets because they understood the danger of a bullet. Usually they left us to face those bullets on our own.

A few days later my five friends and I were transferred to the fifth battalion, and when our new commanding officer, Stephen Kashaka, saw us he ordered two of my friends to join his platoon bodyguard. Many of the officers liked to have children as their bodyguards because they acted without asking questions. And they were loyal to their Afandes. We were involved in everything – killing and torture was the most exciting job for many of us. We thought it was the way to please our commanding officers.

We would increase our brutality towards our prisoners just to get rank, which meant more recognition and authority. But we were too young to realise what we did to the enemy would haunt our dreams and thoughts forever, no matter where we were. We committed terrible acts to please our leaders, and in return they betrayed us. I guess they never thought of us as getting older, or of what would become of us. I suppose they knew we were unlikely to survive the frontline. We had to endure much more than most adults ever see in a lifetime.

Our memories were filled up so quickly with horrors that only human beings are capable of doing and old people grew inside us, like fire under the desperate control of our commanders. Our own minds were often reduced to the basic feelings of thirst and hunger, cold and warmth, and many acted like robots that did only what our new creators desired. If we were meant to be "out of order", we were sent to the frontline to die, sending our memories into oblivion.

So many of us disappeared just like that, and we would forget most deeds worth remembering within a week. I often watched the senior officers, trying to see whether they gave a damn about us or not. I discovered that most of them only cared about their own survival and were trying to see how and when they could take over the government.

In their eyes I saw only the promise of a victorious future filled with wealth and power. It was then I realised that we children did not exist in our leaders' hearts, not even inside Museveni's.

The Fate of Two Friends

ONE AFTERNOON I WAS SITTING IN THE SHADOW under a tree with my friends. We were talking about our experiences when a parade was called. A commander from another unit stood in front and two platoons were told to march and I happened to be in one of them. We were told that we would be taken to join a new unit, which would attack Simba battalion in western Uganda. When we arrived, I felt my misery disappear because I saw the smiles of my old friends Narongo and Mukombozi. I regained my confidence and strength as I greeted them with their arms around me. I wondered what I would have done without these two women because at that moment everything else seemed cruel and ugly.

The trucks captured from the governmental ministry of works were lined up in front of us, and we were given instructions. I stood there with the gun on my shoulder and listened to our Chihanda, who was buried deep in the glories of war. We were ordered to jump into the trucks, and soon we began singing and shouting so that we could keep up the good morale that we had gained from his words. The journey began – a serious one that gave me the feeling that many of us wouldn't survive. I was extremely scared and looked around trying to find a pair of eyes less scared than mine, but I never found them. Many of us were crying. We were packed close together and the air was dense, just like our mood.

Our senior officers were Fred Rwigyema and Julius Chihanda. Rwigyema was loved by many. He was tall, handsome and a great commander who didn't only persuade us to die for the glory, but also reminded us of the importance of staying alive. On the way we disarmed a police post and the men gave up without firing a single shot.

We continued our journey for most of the day but after Kamwenge we found a place to camp until dawn. Many people came to our camp to greet us and spoke sweet words to us. We watched them sing "We love you liberators". Even the children were excited to see us and many people brought gifts and food for us – but sadly we weren't allowed to accept anything.

I felt proud and so did my comrades, and I began to realise that we meant more to these civilians than to most of our commanders and leaders. It was time to leave again, and our plans had for some reason changed. The original plan had been to leave a couple of hours earlier to attack a sleeping enemy camp, but it was now morning with a rising sun in the sky.

Simba barracks was situated on a hill, close to the main road. We arrived, cut the fence and seconds later, both sides started shooting. We killed most of our enemy who had been inside the barracks. Others were busy charging the dead, while we checked on our casualties. As some of us cried over our lost friends, a new surprise attacker started shooting at us from the other side of the hill.

Everyone ran for cover. Many of our comrades were shot in the back in this first confusion of running for their lives. Still, we kept on fighting with one spirit. Mukombozi wasn't able to take cover because she would shoot the RPG from her hip, and this day it proved to be fatal. Mukombozi was killed by a gun on an anti-personnel vehicle.

When Narongo saw what had happened, she climbed into a tree and began shooting. Rwigyema ordered her down, but she refused. No one saw her body falling, but when we withdrew, we discovered Narongo was missing. When I realised these two women had died, I felt like running away to my father's home, miles away from where we were. Then I thought of what his reaction might be when he saw me in uniform with a gun on my shoulder. Would he scream or kneel down and beg for forgiveness?

Many of us were terrified as we walked down the hillside towards the main road, and saw blood running like little rivers and being sucked into the thirsty ground.

But as always, all we could do was to blink and swallow the pain. Some of our comrades continued to a place called Nyamitanga, while others were ordered to stay behind to take over Simba barracks. It seemed that there was another more feared front, a barracks called Masaka. We hijacked some trucks in a small town called Biharwe, and some of us jumped aboard. A few managed to sing and laugh – some of us had stopped being afraid of death.

My mind was on my home town which I once again left behind, and I wondered whether I would ever return to it. When the word "death" appeared in my mind, I was afraid. I stood up and tried to grab hold of something in the moving truck. My head was spinning. I began to sing like a proud man, with joy in my voice, and soon everybody joined in, and I could see smiling faces around me. We continued until we reached a small trading centre and we were allowed out of the truck.

A few minutes passed and civilians appeared, first slowly and cautiously and then in great numbers. They didn't pay the grown-ups much attention but they tried to give us food and money. None of us were allowed to accept anything because Museveni wanted his soldiers to be different to Dr Obote's. I was offered money but was afraid to accept it in front of anyone. Instead I told the woman to follow me around the corner. I wouldn't have refused the money because I was already a chain smoker.

I hid the money and ran back to where the rest of my comrades stood. Hours later we clashed with government soldiers who were on their way to Simba barracks in Mbarara. The government soldiers lost and withdrew. We joined the mobile brigade commanded by Salem Saleh a day or two later.

The next mission was to attack Masaka barracks. When we arrived, the enemy was on high alert to defend their barracks. The shooting erupted and soon both sides were losing men.

The enemy fought as if they had an endless supply of soldiers and because the barracks was on a hilltop it gave them a good spot from which to fire on us.

I was getting "drunk" on gun smoke, making it impossible to see whether my bullets were killing the enemy or not. All I could see were the dead bodies from both sides. One thing I promised myself was never to get up and pretend that I was bullet-proof. I took cover, always shooting when I was hidden on the ground, and when an enemy fell I would convince myself it was my gun that had killed them. The battle went on for much longer than I expected, even with the much-feared fifth battalion on our side.

The enemy's bullets fell on us like hail and we had to retreat. Running away, everything I owned felt as heavy as boulders, and I thought of throwing my Uzi gun away only that was a serious offence, so I began with my cap. But it did nothing, I still felt heavy. Soon we came to a place where nothing was worth running away from. Some comrades lay down under the trees, and those who had cigarettes smoked, while others cleaned their guns. I asked one of my comrades for a cigarette and he told me to pay for it. I went for the money in my pockets but I had thrown them away. I thought of telling him but became afraid, imagining they would call me a coward.

A few hours later, at our rally point, the briefing began. This time it was from Salem. He told us that there was nothing else we could do but continue until we had taken over the barracks. We would attack again, and this time we could not afford to lose. Within a few days, the enemy was losing strength and the NRA had captured most barracks and other key positions. During this time more and more government soldiers wanted to join us – only a few lucky ones were to join our side.

The NRA wanted to seal off Katonga Bridge, so we were told we were to join the fifth and first battalions. When I heard this my spirit rose because I was expecting to meet my friends once again. When the fifth battalion arrived, we were told that senior officer Kashaka had left the unit to get revenge on his father's killers. I was so disappointed because I wouldn't see any of my friends though I kept hoping that one day I would get to see those who were Kashaka's bodyguards.

The fifth battalion now had a new commander, Ahmad Kashilingi, who had been appointed by Museveni after Kashaka left. Kashilingi was a Munyankole and a former Idi Amin soldier. He was well trained in combat and in administration, and tall enough to look a giraffe in the eyes. He had a beard that gave him the nickname Kalevu, meaning "goat's beard".

He had a history of being clever enough to escape the most notorious prison in Uganda, called Luzira, where he was kept when Idi Amin's government had been overthrown by Museveni and Dr Obote. Kashilingi was well respected and feared by most other senior officers. The fifth battalion had the greatest fighters. Moses Drago, M Kanabi and Julius Bruce. These young boys were of Baganda origin. Death seemed to be the only way in which they would be separated. Among these fighters Moses Drago caught my attention. He was one of the youngest ranked officers.

Soon we were ordered to march alongside one another. The fifth battalion was ordered to be on the ready because we would soon advance and cross a small, heavily-guarded bridge, Katonga Bridge, a few kilometres from Kampala, the capital.

At the parade we were told that the Mobile Brigade was doing such a good job that soon they would take over the capital. Now that I had survived two major battles, I knew I had a big chance of seeing this city which most of us kids could only dream of. Before we left for Katonga we obtained a lot of brand new cars. I saw officers knocking over expensive cars, men who didn't even know how to start them.

Was this really what we had been fighting for, I asked myself, watching the senior officers doing the same, running up and down with women who were wild about these new freedom fighters. The soldiers had not washed for days. I suppose these women were perfectly unaware of it, or perhaps they just enjoyed the smell. All of this happened in a small town named Lukaya.

I watched all of this madness while my comrades and I relaxed under a tree. Three fat women approached us. They invited us to a nearby bar and took me for being a boy too. I enjoyed being seen as a boy, so I told my comrades not to say anything about my true identity.

We drank what they offered us and it was the first time any of us had tasted alcohol. All the people in the bar were crazy with excitement about our presence. We laughed and laughed, looking at their gestures as they eagerly offered us drinks. We didn't care whether we got drunk or not because we knew our leaders had no time left to see what we were up to. We were getting drunk and the women began to touch us. Whenever my woman got too close to the truth, I removed her hand. She laughed at me, and assured everybody that I was afraid of women.

My comrades burst into laughter, although I noticed they too were afraid. I wanted to see the minds of these strange beings so I was patient. The women were wild and tried with more strength to touch us between our legs. When this happened all of us got angry. We stood up, pointed our guns at the shocked women and forced them to raise their arms above their heads. At that moment a soldier walked into the bar. I noticed his mouth open and close in surprise before he spun around and disappeared.

A minute later he returned with a drunk commander. We began to laugh when we saw him swaying from side to side, telling us to leave the stupid civilians alone. On our way out he asked why we were in such a situation and we explained that these women wanted to rape us. He was satisfied with that because he knew our only strength was our guns. Suddenly he sat down in the middle of the street laughing, pointing at me. "Did they even want to rape China?" When he had finished rolling around with laughter we moved on to another bar, where a lot of women went wild there too. The commander enjoyed telling everyone how terrified we were of the women.

I was thinking about my mother – whether she did the same things as these women. Anger grew inside my stomach, and suddenly I felt like shutting everybody up with my gun. I left the bar and sat myself against a tree watching the nightlife. Everyone except me seemed to have found a partner, and the loneliness seemed to have been made only for me.

We stayed in Lukaya for a short time, enjoying our time away from the war. At the parade we were told to bear in mind that we might be needed at any time and afterwards my comrades and I discussed our previous battle. We assured each other no battle could be as big as the last one. We would survive many more.

We agreed that no other frontline could ever frighten us again – we were real fighters now. Then a message came from Museveni or Saleh. Senior officer and commander of fifth battalion, Ahmad Kashilingi, was ordered to take us across Katonga and capture Entebbe International Airport. We were briefed and told to prepare ourselves for a morning attack.

I was one of the first who was ready with my Uzi on my shoulder. Worried and excited, I watched the sun rise while the drivers ran around looking for which trucks to drive. Most of them had glowing red eyes, and I knew they had been drinking all night. Nearly everyone was ready to go. Then I saw a terrible sight. The commanders, including our battalion commander, were all drunk – Muslims and non-Muslims alike. We went to Katonga but couldn't go ahead with the attack. Big guns were lined up behind the bridge, ready to tear us to pieces. We were ordered to dig in so we began digging holes in which to take cover. As I dug I remembered I had promised myself never to judge a situation before it happened. The only thing separating us from the enemy that day was the river that only a fool would think of crossing under fire.

Later that day both sides started firing, though neither side took the initiative to cross the narrow bridge, which I am sure, every soldier considered suicide.

We were stuck at Katonga for about four months, until Kashilingi was ordered to cross the waters – within hours. I looked at our side and saw nothing as large as their weapons on the other side. At first I couldn't believe the order was real, but I couldn't have heard incorrectly. Museveni and his brother were the only ones who could give orders like that one. He knew very well how devastating this could be and I began to think he was being careless with our lives.

I wondered whether he would keep any of the promises he made when he was a hopeful rebel. We moved over the bridge, and we were falling like flies, but the commander shouted at us to move. We continued through bullets and hand grenades. Suddenly one of my friends nicknamed "Strike Commando" went down. He shouted, begging for help, but not one of us could stop to help him. We managed to push the enemy back but we lost many soldiers. I walked among the casualties, looking for my friend. When I went to see the dead I was interrupted by angry comrades who raged at the bodies of the enemy with fists and boots.

I could not cry even though I knew my friend was dead. I couldn't cry for fear of breaking down. I had come this far, though I never seemed to harden. It was strange to see children with a lust for killing and torturing. They could even smile after a "rare killing", competing to earn nicknames like Commando, Rambo and Suicide. I hated feeling sorry for others, even the enemy. I had crossed the line. I had used up both hands to count my fallen friends.

Now it was time to decide. I was broken, but I was still kind and unselfish. Now I thought I needed to be a strong, full-blooded killer – if I only could.

Soon every child carried more than three magazines tied to their AK47, and soon many of us had up to six magazines each. I guess we all felt that being seen with so many magazines would impress our leaders. We forgot about our shoulders and soon many of us started walking like old men.

All of us needed someone to love us and if your parents haven't given you love, who will? Some children's parents were dead, and those who were alive had let us down. Now we had to search for love from strangers and they too looked the other way. We were on our own, and we were forced to find love and compassion in the wrong places. We were forced to get love from a gun.

We were told our guns were our mothers, our friends, our whole world, and we must rather lose ourselves than our guns. At night our leaders would come and steal the guns from us, and the next day they would ask us where our guns were. You would look everywhere and they would beat you and roll you in the mud, accusing you of giving your gun to rebels or, they would say you had sold it. After the beatings, they would give you your gun and say to you: "That's what happens when you lose your mother." Whenever I went to sleep I wound my gun belt around my neck. Still, I was afraid to fall asleep.

I'm convinced Museveni knew about our treatment because he too had a child as his bodyguard. Fred Kayanja was one of the children we were with in the bush, and he became Museveni's bodyguard when he was about ten years old. When I ran away from Uganda he was still Museveni's bodyguard. Many of our leaders behaved like crazy people, and Museveni loved them and hated the good ones. Many of the good senior officers who had power to change things were dying in car accidents or of AIDS. The mad officers were promoted rapidly – it didn't matter what they did. The good officers were always jailed, and all bad leaders had all the power.

Once again we had to leave. We were driven along the blood-stained main road. Bodies were scattered everywhere, dogs were eating some of them but I watched without any feelings, remembering how they had just killed my friend.

On our short cut to Entebbe a helicopter attacked us. We were better equipped now, shooting at them with a 37-calibre artillery gun, and soon they retreated to the Victoria Nile. We carried on fighting and when we were told that Kampala was only a few miles away, we were filled with hope and saw the future promised to us.

After a few days we faced a strong and well-equipped enemy. They seemed as if they were all prepared to die. Kashilingi begged for reinforcements though no one came to our rescue. "Let not one of you die here – fight and defend yourselves!" he commanded. Weeks later the enemy had retreated and I could see hope in all our faces.

It was a surprise that some of us had survived. The NRA had lost so many great senior officers. It seemed as if we had killed them ourselves becasue we feared them. Weeks later we marched past the retreating enemy and their precious belongings they had dropped along the way. I was surprised our soldiers passed it all without picking up anything, but I could see a light of glory in every eye. I guessed that now Kampala belonged to us and a life without guns was about to begin. I smiled as I remembered Museveni's promise to us.

On the road an uneasy crowd of civilians stopped us. They saw us as saviours and pointed towards a house further down the street. A girl from the crowd threw herself in front of our platoon commander, Julius Bruce, and begged him to rescue her parents. Others followed and a split second later, everyone was shouting, making the situation unbearable. Bruce spoke with a man from the crowd and shortly after he gave us a short briefing before ordering us to storm the house. We disarmed the enemy without firing a single shot. A group of exhausted people had been locked up in one of the rooms.

When everything had calmed down another fear rose inside me. The enemy soldiers terrified me. Very few of us were even near their height, and their faces had numbers tattooed on their faces. I stood there with my Uzi in front of an unarmed enemy, ready to pee in my pants. Some began questioning the hostage-takers, while others secured the house. We walked through the rooms stepping over dead bodies, some of which had been there for days. We couldn't count all the bodies because of the smell. We left the enemy to their fate. The civilians tore them apart. These men had been hiding behind those walls for several days, killing men, women, and children. I asked myself how, if these men really had hearts, could they stay in a house with that stench, one that could even suffocate a pig?

In Kampala, raging civilians were chasing government soldiers, and everybody ran around in chaos. The street was on fire with our enemy's screams. They were burned on car tires, but there was nothing we could do about it. We just walked through the streets pretending everything was in order.

When we arrived in the inner city, I couldn't see anything like the impressive descriptions I had heard. But before I could feel too disappointed we were overrun by thousands of happy citizens. Some were crying, others knelt down to thank us.

For the first time on Ugandan soil women were armed and walked as proudly as any man. Many looked as if they had forgotten the war, which was replaced by bright eyes of hope, and I couldn't feel that way. I couldn't loosen up because I knew there was more to come. I had learned never to feel secure until I could see the next valley or look around the next corner.

Part Four

Survival

Escaping the Battlefield

TO SOME OF US THE DISAPPOINTMENT came as lightning from the sky. We learned that our battalion had to push the enemy northwards.

I didn't know whether I was disappointed or relieved when Kashilingi handed over command to senior officer Julius Ayine. Kashilingi had been part of those who created the NRA. He was a proud man who was known as a hard lion. For some reason the Bagandas loved him, and his entire bodyguard platoon was of that tribe.

Ayine was a Hima, from the same tribe as Museveni. He was a good commander and he had a reputation for protecting his men on the battlefield.

The frontline had already moved to northern Uganda. At Kafu Bridge we met strong resistance and I shook with fear that I wouldn't survive another battle. Pictures of the horrors I had seen at Katonga flashed through my mind – the hopeless standoff that lasted for days and the death of my treasured friend.

After some days we continued to a bridge at Karuma. I saw a bridge that was still untouched by war and thick bush covering a heavy flood passing beneath it. I asked myself why, after we had taken Kampala, were we still fighting? We had been promised another life after overthrowing the government in Kampala. I hadn't seen anyone relieved from duty so far, and I sensed that if I wanted another life, I would have to give it to myself. I decided to survive by escaping this battle. I somehow had to get sick. I asked for a cigarette and had it, ran to my platoon sergeant and threw up.

I told him I had malaria. When he didn't find any difference between his temperature and mine, he told me that I was lying. "So you want me to send you back to headquarters?" He said he wouldn't. Not ready to give up, I went to a friend of mine who was good at making clever plans. I took him aside and he told me that I had to drink my urine to get a fever. I thought he was joking.

But when you are desperate you will try anything. I decided to try. I went to a deserted spot and filled a cup with urine. I thought about it once more before deciding to drink – on the count of three. When the first drops reached my stomach, I threw everything up. When I was on my feet again I was overwhelmed with anger. I ran straight to the trickster to tear him to pieces with my hands. The children around us cheered while I bit and scratched him as much as I could. After a while, a mutual and older comrade jumped in and pushed us apart. I broke down, making the mistake of telling him what had happened right in front of everybody.

Before I had finished explaining, almost everyone there was laughing, even the mediator. I was furious and ran away to sit alone with my embarrassment. Everything seemed hopeless. Soon the trickster came to me and sat down. As I looked down, thinking about whether to forgive him or not, he apologised and gave me a hug, saying he had meant me no harm.

In the Money

THE FOLLOWING MORNING I DISCOVERED that one of the trucks was going to Kampala. I told the driver my story and he decided to help me. Early the next morning I waited at a safe distance from the base. When I was in the truck, I felt as though I was in heaven, feeling safe for the first time since joining the NRA. Then the nightmares began. I sensed I had been screaming when I felt a gentle push on my head. With my backpack on I jumped out of the truck, and I was left on the road to wander on my own.

I drifted through Kampala feeling deserted and alone. It was extremely hot and the only relief were the shadows of the hard walls I passed, keeping out any unwanted souls. I wished more than ever to have a place I could call home. I heard a hooter and looked up. Puzzled, I walked towards the car with a feeling that the signal was meant for somebody else. A fat middle-aged Mugandan woman looked straight at me from behind the wheel. I pointed at my chest with my eyebrows raised, and when she nodded I hurried towards her.

I got into the car and saw the streets pass by but then I turned my head. She had a sweaty face and a big stomach and I could tell that she had had a bad day as she struggled against the heat. I almost snapped when she said she loved me and said I was welcome in her home. "She must be crazy," I thought, but since I needed somewhere to sleep, I accepted her invitation without concern. I sat on one of her sofas looking at her collection of furniture and things I thought only presidents had.

When she came back from changing her clothes she asked me to accompany her on a trip into town. I agreed and grabbed my bag, refusing to leave it behind because I didn't want her to know I carried a loaded gun. As we drove she proudly told me she was a business-woman. When we returned she hurried over to my side and showed me some photos of herself in foreign countries.

I noticed her taking a sip from a bottlefor every photo she showed me – there were many empties on the table already. Soon she was all over me. I jumped and shouted, "Get off me!" I was angry. I tried to control myself by drinking more beer. Luckily, before I was too dizzy, the food arrived on the table. We had without talking much but when I had finished my meal she annoyed me again. I opened my backpack and drew my gun. The house girls screamed once before I ordered all three of them to shut up. I told the woman to give me her money, and she panicked, jumping right over to a drawer. I stood with the money in my hands not knowing what to do. This had definitely not been what I wanted but there was no turning back, so I kept pointing the gun at them until I realised I could just walk away. I warned them not to follow me. I was trembling with fear when I left. I stood there for a short while, coughing to assure them that I was still there. Then I climbed the gate and walked towards the city, ready to fight off any threat.

On my way I met a group of people. I asked them how to find the bus park. They tried to explain but they only confused me. I asked them to show me where to go and they showed me to the minibus – an old Hiace filled to the brim with people. Just before Mbarara, our taxi was stopped at a roadblock. Bruce, the roadblock commander, knew me well and wanted to know where I was going. I pretended not to know, so he ordered the taxi to leave without me. He invited me to a bar not far from his post, and with a smile I agreed to go.

In the toilet I counted my money. It was enough to help track down the woman I once denied to be my mother. Bruce and I stayed in the bar for the rest of that evening, eating and talking about wars and friends lost in battles. Later we went to the barracks and I was shown where to sleep, only I couldn't fall asleep because my father's house was only a short distance away from the barracks. I felt a lust for revenge for quite some time, and it seemed the right moment to take my tormentors out of my life forever.

With my gun I went to my old school and looked up the hill at my father's house. My stomach hurt and I ground my teeth whenever I thought of any of them. Then my trigger finger would itch. I wanted to walk up the hill and shoot him and his wife, but when I finally decided to go, my body froze like a soldier disobeying his superior. I was angry with myself. I stayed there for about an hour, crying. Finally I returned to the barracks where I found Bruce looking for me. With anger I told him of my desire and I could feel my heart hit my chest with every word I uttered.

After listening he put his arm around my shoulder, and together we walked towards a rock and sat down. He told me he had a bad father too, but he wasn't going to kill him. "Why?" I interrupted.

"Because then there would be no difference between us – both of us would be bad men," he replied. I listened carefully to his words and I found them perfectly sensible. I wasn't like my father and would never want to be. I assured him that everything about killing my family was forgotten, and he nodded, smiling sadly. The next day I told him I would go and look for my mother.

Mother

I HAD RUN AWAY FROM MY UNIT when the war was still on and to be safe, I decided to wear civilian clothes. I put my gun in a bag and began my journey. I found absolutely nobody at my mother's house – the place was deserted. I was disappointed, and I needed to get myself together before making another move. I had been sitting there for a while when I realised I had left my bag in the bus. I realised the only thing of any value to me was my gun. When I realised it was gone it seemed as though I had lost myself.

Now I needed my mother more than ever. I went back to the town square. I sat down and thought about what had passed since I had run from her. Everything seemed to have started that night when I left her house, and I couldn't help wondering what my life might have been like if I had stayed with her.

I stood up when I saw a woman coming in my direction. Her face changed into one big smile when I asked her about my mother. She took me by the hand, assuring me I would see her again. As I entered a house I saw a girl sitting on a chair who looked exactly like my sister, Margie. She looked at me, and looked back with a thoughtful expression on her face, but as I came closer she looked up again. Suddenly Margie jumped out of her chair and cried out my name. But I remained standing, embarrassed and too proud to fall around her neck. She grabbed my hand and dragged me through the house and out again at lightning speed.

Now I was so confused that I just followed her up the street, but before long I saw my mother in front of us, walking slowly. When we stopped she only looked at us and said, "Let's go home!"

The three of us sat in front of the house for a while and they began questioning me. Margie was more interested in how I had got into the army than in my sudden disappearance years ago.

My mother told me that the only reason for her staying in town was to make sure I could find her again one day. During all that time she had been living with one burning question – why I had run away that night. For the first time in my life I looked my mother in the eye and told her the truth. I felt silly about that evening when I had thought they were going to eat me. She laughed and I suppose the reason I had given was strange.

My sister looked at me with narrow eyes and smiled before she told me it was probably a wise decision after all because one never knew what our mother was up to. I didn't really know my mother but I got to know her quite quickly. She had funny ways of expressing herself, using little stories. You were never sure whether they were true or not but they would make you happy. I remember my sister and I laughing our heads off when she told us that the Pope's mother was a Tutsi and his father an Italian.

There were things that a woman of her age shouldn't eat, but she had everything. When you asked her why she would only say, "I will eat everything that was created before me!" Everyone around her, young and old, were fond of her.

But I still couldn't find love in my heart after I found my mother, even though she gave me lots of it. The period of time from when I ran from my mother had been hard for her too. Her husband, the former chief of the village, had passed away. Everything they once possessed had been looted during the change of government. All she had left was a small rented room, and she was selling homemade liquor to earn a living. I could not feel at home there.

To be Seen

I WANTED TO STAY WITH MY MOTHER, despite how I felt, only the people around me didn't see me as the person I wanted them to see. I believed I was above any civilian, giving me the final say on everything, though no one was willing to let me. Since I had lost my gun I could not return to the NRA, and my past had to remain a secret. My sister insisted I start school, though I didn't know if I wanted to go back to school. But my life was in their hands, so I had to do it their way.

Margie made sure that I started school before she returned to Kampala. Every day after school I fought and for some reason it was always the older children who annoyed me. I lost most of the fights, although I didn't know how to stop. My mother would ask me, "Why are you bleeding?" I never answered because I thought she was too fragile to take my pain. I was seen as a mad child.

No one seemed able to help me, and of course, I never asked for any either. I believed anything that concerned me was for me to deal with. My mother had no idea how to help me so she sent me to live with a couple she knew through her deceased husband. There I faced more abuse, but still I kept silent and endured it for two months. I returned to my mother, left school and spent my time walking around like an animal in a cage. I had to get out. I had to do something.

I could see the confusion in my mother's eyes, and finally I decided to relieve her of the burden. I started to work as a house girl for a captain and his wife, and after a short period of time I began to see that this wasn't the answer either. I couldn't take it any more. I left because I felt humiliated and I saw this as a step down in my life. I was broken, although I hadn't given up yet. The beatings and pain inflicted by my father and stepmother had made me strong and I had learned never to give up.

Once more I returned to my mother who took me in with open arms. Suddenly I realised that I would have to start my life all over again if I wanted to make it. But there was no turning back. I saw that my childhood had vanished and I couldn't fit in with civilian life. I needed an identity and the only place I felt I could find it again was back in the army. I realised that I simply didn't fit into this community, being a small girl with a vast military experience. I hardly knew anything but the life of a soldier, so I decided to try again as a recruit. I had spent three years away from the army.

There were trucks driving around recruiting anyone who wanted to join the NRA. When the truck I was on was full it drove off to Nyakyishara. Training was even quicker than I had expected, and in a month's time most of us were taken direct to the frontline. I had learned ways to get around the system, so I managed to avoid this. The instructors thought I was amazing because I knew everything they taught us, and before the training was over, the officer in charge had promoted me to the rank of lance corporal – I was only 13 years old.

I joined the forty-fifth battalion and stayed there for some time before I let my mother know where I was. My conscience had been worrying me and I felt bad that she had to buy milk when my father had an entire farm full of cows. I decided to pay my father a visit.

My stepsisters and brothers seemed to have missed me. They welcomed me with lots of love. They escorted me the rest of the way to my father, who was relaxing in the garden on a comfortable chair. For a couple of seconds he froze, his blinking eyes the only moving part of him. I stood there for the first time since I was a small child. Suddenly, with a loud and desperate voice, he blurted out, "Baby!" and clumsily jumped to his feet to give me a hug. I remained as still as dead wood.

With a face filled with despair he turned around without looking at me and went into the house in a dizzy walk. To my surprise he returned with a chair and placed it beside his as in a ceremony of respect. We sat there for a while without a word as I waited for my father to begin and for my stepmother to come and greet me. When she suddenly did, I just managed to control the anger bursting out of my chest, and I greeted her with a forced smile. Now my father relaxed as though we had always been friends, excitedly asking me about when I joined the army. I caught myself looking at him with angry eyes. He shied away with a fake smile when I told him that a civilian was not entitled to such information from a soldier, and there was silence. I rejected a glass of milk from my stepmother's hands, telling her I had already eaten. The truth was I still didn't trust her.

That same day I went back, still angry. I had never forgotten my father's cruelty – when he had chosen my goats to be slaughtered one by one. Maybe he thought he'd taught me some kind of lesson. I didn't know, but I decided to teach him a lesson and maybe help my mother at the same time.

It was morning and I was sitting outside my quarters on the lawn. My battalion had a good time, often hanging around the barracks on standby for whatever might happen. I had had a few problems with certain soldiers in our battalion. One of them happened to cross my path that morning while I was relaxing by myself with my Uzi at my side. This tormentor approached me arrogantly, with his face raised as if he was the president himself. He wanted to sit there on the exact spot where I was sitting. He told me to move. Distracted and annoyed, I looked up at him – I very much wanted to punch his nose hard, but he was much older and stronger than me. I asked him why he didn't choose another place to sit. He didn't reply. Instead he began to pull me up by my arm and then he sat down. Then he told me to respect him, even though we had the same rank – lance corporal. Now my blood was boiling and my loaded gun was in my hands. Still he said, as if he were a wise old man, that more age earned more respect. Through my clenched teeth I told him to move if he didn't want a bullet from my gun. He ignored my warning.

I watched him struggle to get back on his feet, screaming with pain. He had blood gushing everywhere from the wound, and then the RPs were all over me. I did as I was ordered, handing over my Uzi. They took the boy to the sick-bay. I was taken to the second in command. I told him this child had deliberately annoyed me from the day I joined the battalion.

After my explanation he ordered the two RPs to drag me through a mud pit, until I looked like a wild little pig. Then they brought me back through the barracks by the most trafficked route. Now I had even more time on my own. The commander had confiscated my gun for a month without sending me to jail, and there wasn't much to do as a soldier without a weapon. I decided to pay my father another visit.

When I arrived at the taxi park I bumped into my father. He was in an unusual mood, wanting to talk. I, however, was busy with plans and I tried to cut him off with short replies.

Suddenly he said something that struck me like lightning. He asked me when I was going to visit my grandmother at the farm. "If you could just look into my mind, father," I thought, and I left him without an answer. Then I went to the minibus, and waited for it to fill up. I wondered if I had forgotten anything in my plan, and as we got near the farm, at around twelve o'clock, I was going over each step in my mind.

I got off the minibus and walked through the old dust trail that led to the farm. I could almost see the farmhouse when I met the manager of the neighbouring farm. We knew each other from when I was a little child. He came to me and hugged me and pulled my uniform. "You're a big girl now,!" he said, though my rubber boots went far above my knees. "Hey, you're a soldier now!" He still had his bushy hair that he probably hadn't combed since I'd seen him the last time, and he was as tall as ever.

When I was about to step onto my father's land, I was certain nothing could go wrong. My brother stood outside the house with a pack of dogs, already looking at me as I eyed him. My heart beat faster and faster as I realised how much I had missed him. He acted so cool – he just looked at me as though I'd returned from a trip in the bush but I didn't mind. I ran to him and gave him a long hug, holding him until he finally returned my feelings by laying his head on my shoulder. After having talked for a minute or two, Grandmother came outside and hugged me. Immediately she invited me inside with the same old hanging face, with her unusual smile.

Before I could finish the meal Grandmother had served, my brother was at the door. We went with his dogs to hunt, as we had done so many times before in our childhood, before the war of my life. It felt good to walk beside my big brother again, but as we walked I noticed he was eager to say something. He wanted to know why I had returned, and I replied that our mother wanted me to take some cows for her. "You mean that you came here to steal?" he asked. "Yes," I answered. His only reply was, "Then you are stupid not to bring your gun."

We began our hunting mission and, happy with his reaction to my planned revenge, I enjoyed every second of it. Half the day had passed and we were getting tired. The dogs seemed disappointed too, picking on each other while looking at their master with embarrassed eyes. We debated our hunt on the way home, like friends discussing a football match. We knew there was plenty of meat waiting for us at the farm. I went straight to my grandmother followed by an excited and curious brother who sat in a corner as I approached her. She looked up from her dishes and I told her I was sent by my father to make sure a lorry was loaded with eight cows and seven goats, and to bring it to him. She asked why my father didn't come himself and, always ready with an answer which my army training had taught me, I told her a soldier in the truck would save him from having to bribe the traffic police. Furthermore, I said, he'd told me to choose the very finest animals.

It was hard for me to see if she had bought my lie. She nodded with an angry face. My careless brother was laughing. While we had supper the manager arrived as promised. He had seen my father in town and had told him about my visit. Finally the man stood up and walked to the door. Then he turned around and said, "By the way, he's coming to visit tomorrow morning." My last hope withered when my grandmother turned to look at me. All the love she had shown me during the day was now gone.

My heart skipped a few beats. My grandmother assured me my father would kill me for being a common thief. I couldn't breathe. I knew I had to escape immediately. She kept on scaring me until my brother shouted at her to leave me alone. He stood up as if nothing had been said, and whispered in my ear to remind me of my confiscated gun. Then he went to bed.

It was five o'clock in the morning when I got dressed. My brother was in a bed across the room. I thanked him in silence for the night before. A few seconds later I was walking quickly towards the main road. I turned away from the dust trail and headed through the bush. As I left the trail I felt the creepy hands of panic on my back, and the adrenaline in my chest.

At the main road I caught a lift with a Somalian petrol tanker. The drivers looked weary after a long drive, talking to me so they could stay awake.

Just as we arrived at the place where my battalion was stationed, a new problem emerged and I had to make up my mind fast. I knew that my father wouldn't back off. He would have me reported as a thief to the battalion commander. I decided to go with the Somalians to Kabale, where I knew a detach commander who had been stationed there to stop the smuggling from Uganda to Rwanda.

Nakasongora

HE REMEMBERED ME AND TOOK ME into his detachment that was there to stop and search vehicles for goods. Soon I learned that soldiers took the money the state never paid them. I started to earn money, allowing smugglers to cross the border. I didn't know what to do with my money because I had never earned any, but I loved chicken. I spent all my money on chicken without thinking about the future. I thought I would be there forever but I was mistaken. Before I could get too used to my new life, all of us were taken back to battalion headquarters.

There we found senior officer David Tinyefunza, who had been sent there by the army chief, Elly Tumwine. He told our unit we were getting fat and corrupt, and to end this he was sending us to a place named Nakasongora, right in the middle of the bush. The only things in this area were the ruined buildings, bombed during the war with Tanzania. It was a godforsaken place.

Speaking in harsh words, without looking at us, he ordered the officers to train us hard from six o'clock in the morning until six in the evening. He promised to stay and monitor our training for six months, until we had to move on. After turning his eyes to our sorry line of faces he said this was what to expect for acting like non-soldiers. Tinyefunza's words were as harsh as the place, and I knew this wasn't just our training. It was one of those crucial times in one's life when the wrong word would end it all. Tinyefunza was a brutal man and those of us who knew him well would never even look into his eyes as he spoke.

Tinyefunza was one of those senior officers who terrified all of us. Soldiers and junior officers were even more frightened of him when we heard rumours that he had tied up some junior officers and shot them because he thought they were cowards.

We had many brutal officers. I remember one whose name was Suicide. He was a war hero, a mad one. Suicide had the power to do anything. He could rape civilian and army girls and nothing would happen to him because he was a good soldier. He did everything by force. Our souls belonged to our instructors, and if we wanted them back, we had to pay a heavy price. They had many ways to make you suffer, but most of their torture seemed reserved for female soldiers. The older girls had more problems than all the other soldiers because they had to pay with their own bodies. The instructors had power, and since most of the officers were doing the same, there was no one to stop them. We female soldiers had to offer sex to more than five officers in one unit. Nearly every evening an officer would come and order you to report to his place, usually at 9pm. It would have been a little easier on us if it had been one or two afandes, but every day in the week we had to sleep with different afandes against our will! If we refused our afandes' orders, we would have to say goodbye to visiting our families. On top of that, the abuse would turn violent and we would get extra duties. After seven days without proper sleep you could even fall asleep on parade. We lived in fear all day, thinking about 9pm in the evening. I remember praying to God, asking him to not let the day end because of that hour.

Perhaps this was a taste of hell. Where else can such pain belong? It was so painful and I could only cry with my heart. I couldn't allow my real tears to flow – tears I would never have survived. Our afandes were always angry, and they seemed too cold to see the pain they were causing us. In bed with them it felt as though I was sleeping with death. Our male comrades knew about the abuse. They called us *masala ya makubwa* and *guduria*, the food of the afandes, the "big pot" from which all the officers ate their fill. I started hating myself, blaming myself for having nowhere else to go.

I almost convinced myself that it was a part of nature, that every girl had to endure it. It made me a little stronger when I knew I wasn't alone. The NRA gave us weapons and made us fight their war. They made us hate, kill and torture, and they forced us to sleep with them – we had no choice. Museveni had a choice – but it was to look the other way. Most of the high-ranking officers behaved like madmen. How could Museveni not have seen this?

Museveni should have realised what his monsters were doing to us! Except we weren't his children, so he never gave a damn. One evening, some of us were sitting around the fire resting after a hard day's training. When the training officer told me to follow him, I did so with his bodyguards close behind, and I wondered if I had done something wrong. But when we reached his place, he sent me back to get my belongings. I returned and his chief escort showed me a place to sleep. We called him God, the short form for Godfrey. "God" was thirty years old. He was a strong man, although he had a limp from being shot in the leg. The next day I sat on the bed weary and tired. He came into my room and told me that I had to go with him. I stood up, scared, and followed him.

In the morning he told me to show up in his room every evening, and with terrifying eyes he made it clear it was an order. The only thing I could reply was "Yes, sir." My falling heart made the words dim. He asked me as though he were shouting to a whole line-up of soldiers. I could only nod, and with a weak breath I walked to the morning parade. About three weeks later the battalion got a new commander, captain Sam Waswa Balikarege, and I tried very hard to become friends with one of his escorts. One day his escort told me that Waswa was going to Kampala and I begged him to get me out of Nakasongora. He promised to do his best. In the evening, I met God in the doorway to his room, and he told me to go inside. I stood there for a moment eyeing a bayonet on the floor. I grabbed it and hid it under the mattress.

At the most terrible moment I silently said to him, "I wish you would die in your sleep, you bastard!" All night I was touching the bayonet feeling angry and dirty, but I feared this man too much even though I could have done it in a second. The morning came without sleep and without the job done. I went to Waswa's place and found his bodyguards packing. To my relief the escort told me to get in the car, and soon he jumped behind the wheel and led the convoy out of Nakasongora to Kampala. Finally I was out and the same day after our arrival, I went to my mother's.

When my mother saw me she started to cry and I couldn't understand why. I felt a strange pain inside me, and my anger rose like a charging rhino, making me shout at her. I told her to shut up, that I hated people who cried, especially when it was me they were crying for. I stopped and turned away from her when I saw her shocked face. She wasn't crying, but I still had the same pain inside, feeling low and unworthy.

A month passed. I was getting back my strength, and my thoughts stopped haunting and blaming me. My mother told me she knew an officer, Ronald, whom she thought might be able to "slip" me back into the army. In the evening we went there and met his bodyguard Kusain, a small child who was only nine years old.

Kusain took us to Ronald with small, confident steps. He seemed almost like a man in his finest years. Ronald told us he would soon go back to his unit in the Kabamba training wing, and that I could join his unit there. He promised to pick me up from my mother's when it was time to leave. It must have been the following Thursday, at around two o'clock, when Kusain, Ronald and his wife, Justine, arrived at my mother's. After travelling by bus and train halfway across Uganda we arrived at Kabamba the following morning.

The first week everything was going well for me – but not for Kusain. Every morning Justine beat him for wetting the bed, and Ronald joined in at least once. I felt bad and angry watching Kusain, a soldier, being beaten by a civilian woman. I saw myself in Kusain, just as I had been beaten for wetting my bed. But I was going mad fighting those unwanted memories, and I couldn't help him much. Two more weeks passed and I began to wonder when Ronald was going to give me a post. When I asked, he told me I should stay there as a part of his escort.

I was disappointed because in those four weeks Justine had given Kusain and I a great deal of work I felt wasn't meant for a soldier. There was nothing Justine loved more than to stay in bed. And when she finally tired of doing that, she would bring a chair and sit in front of the house. She would sit for hours looking at her own pretty face in a mirror, mimicking different kinds of screams and other ugly faces. I came to hate her so much I sometimes imagined her being shot. I would have been able to run away to another battalion because no sort of identification had yet been made on the new government army, however, this unit was so tiny that it would have been so easy to spot someone was missing.

Unfortunately, living as Justine's private waitress I had no idea of the kind of hell it was going to be working as Ronald's escort. Justine left to visit her parents, and I was happy at first. Ronald came home and told Kusain to go and borrow some sugar from a neighbour. When Kusain left my heart began to beat in alarm. Ronald asked me if I'd ever slept with anyone. Before I could consider my response, he grabbed me and threw me onto his bed. I cried in desperation but he stopped me with his dirty hand. It seemed to last for an eternity, but when he left I saw that no time had passed. The image of him haunted me like a demon.

When Kusain came back I was sitting on the corner of the bed, crying silent tears as if his hand still covered my mouth. The touch of Kusain's comforting hand on my shoulder made me burst into tears. At first I could not tell him what had happened, only my head and body was aching with bad memories that forced me to tell him. His face changed and had an expression I cannot describe, but I could see he understood more than I had thought. The little Mugandan told me to be strong, even though he was sure that no one would intervene if we spoke about it because he believed that most officers behaved in the very same way. I could not take it anymore and told him I was leaving the next day. I felt sorry to leave Kusain, and advised him to try and find a higher ranked officer to take him as a bodyguard, because then Ronald would be afraid to claim him back.

The following morning I went to one of the instructors just after Ronald left for work. He was a forty-year-old sergeant whom I thought of as a good man. He looked at me with an increasingly troubled face as I told him what had happened. I understood why – he himself was afraid of Ronald. Still, after a couple of minutes he took me to his wife. He told her everything and they decided to hide me. For three days I lived behind a locked door, breathing fresh air through a tiny window. The second day the wife told me not to open the window because Ronald had been looking for me. That day I heard him asking for me and I was terrified when I learned that he wasn't satisfied with their answer. I heard him walk through the house. The last I saw of him were his boots which I saw from under my bed. On the third day the sergeant and his wife gave me some money for transport back to my mother's. He even assigned a recruit to escort me to the train station. We had to walk through the forest to avoid meeting Ronald.

After having walked for a while the recruit talked to me in a strange voice and, terrified, I started walking faster. Suddenly he grabbed me and said if I didn't make love to him he would force me. He tried to justify it saying I had to pay the price for him risking his life. I looked around to find an escape route, a sign of hope, but the forest held everything to itself. I see only glimpses of the sun here and there, and the sound of a scream wouldn't reach further than the next tree.

Nobody would hear me scream for help, and the leaves of the trees just dropped raindrops onto the face of this beast that only deserved the desert.

The things he spoke about on our walk made me question his sanity and I started to think I might die out there. I decided to fight him with my life and dignity. At the last moment I got an idea. I knew that recruits were forbidden to have intercourse before their training was over, so to make him reconsider his decision, I told him I wanted very much to give him what he desired but that he would have to prepare himself to be punished because I had syphilis. He thanked me for my honesty and I just managed to hide my relief. Still, I was shaken when he left me at the station. I cried all the way home, but I smiled to myself thinking how lucky I had been.

Womanhood

WHEN I ARRIVED AT MY MOTHER'S HOUSE she was about to eat supper with a man I did not know. Annoyed, I took her outside and asked her who he was. She smiled and I could see what he meant to her, and I felt disgusted. I told her if she wanted a man I could easily force my father to marry her again. She laughed, saying I was insulting her. Her eyes narrowed when I demanded she chase the man away. Suddenly she shouted at me. She said I had no right to come to her home and chase her visitors away. Her defending him only maddened me more, so I went into the house and told the man myself. He only laughed and said, "These children! When they go to the army they lose all respect for others." When he had finished, my mother sat beside him. I had heard enough, and angered by their determined look, I grabbed the *sigirri*, a small grill, and threw the burning charcoal at them. They screamed in panic as they felt the burning coal inside their clothes. They ran outside jumping around and with a little smile on my face I closed and locked the door. After a while I heard knocking. I got up slowly from where I had been sitting.

My mother begged me to open the door – I told her to sleep at her sweetheart's. Twenty minutes went by before a man presented himself as the landlord. He explained to me that everybody makes mistakes and begged me to let my mother in. She calmed down and told me she had never really liked him anyway. That night I slept like a baby in my mother's arms. It felt good to rest my chin on her breast.

I did not tell her why I had come back – I didn't trust her yet. Besides, I could see she had already struggled enough.

At the beginning of 1988 my mother took me to Kampala to one of her brothers, a man of twenty. He was commanding officer of the 21st battalion, which guarded Entebbe International airport. Caravel seemed very happy to meet me and I hadn't been there for long before I felt at home. My uncle was a very efficient leader with a sharp mind and mouth, and on top of it all he was very handsome. There were always girls swarming around him. I was very happy staying with him.

One day my uncle and I were sitting outside his house talking about this and that while I was playing with his hair. Suddenly a girl appeared, marching very angrily towards us. In a hysterical voice she asked Caravel if this bitch was also his girlfriend. He drew his pistol and shot her in the side of her breast, shouting at her that I happened to be his daughter. The ambulance picked up the bleeding girl, but there was never a charge laid against Caravel.

As time passed I noticed that Caravel's attitude towards me was changing. He began to look at me angrily, telling me he didn't like to see me dressed in military uniform. His words terrified me. I didn't have any idea what other life he expected me to have. I hoped he would stop wanting me out of the army. To make my point, I stopped wearing civilian clothes.

One day when he returned from work he told me to change into civilian clothes. It was time for me to go to school like any other child – I was being sent to my sister, Margie. I wasn't happy with my uncle's decision – I felt devastated. I couldn't trust my sister to take proper care of us after all she had been through. When she arrived I was told to pack my clothes, and I remembered to sneak in a uniform as well.

I saw that I was right. My sister had no shower and the toilet was outside. At night, my sister slept in her bed while I slept on the sofa. The landlady was just like my grandmother, old and mean, and demanded respect. She shouted at me whenever she could. My sister tried to get me into every public school in Kampala, but not one would have me. I was getting fed up with staying home.

I began to gather all the addresses of barracks situated in Kampala, though I had decided to give my sister a second chance. I just had to make sure I could get out of there when I had had enough. A month passed, which to me seemed like years of misery. One morning I woke up after my sister had left for work. I went to bathe myself and noticed something strange. After looking carefully I realised it was blood. I was puzzled because I didn't feel any pain. I tried to think of any time yesterday when I might have sat on something sharp, but couldn't remember anything. I got scared and thought of going to the hospital. Instead I went outside and buried the evidence.

After washing myself I went back to sleep. When I woke up I got a shock. The sofa was turning red too. My sister could be a hard woman, so I decided to run off. I took my secretly packed uniform out of my bag, got dressed and went to the Republic House. There I met with the platoon commander, whom I begged to get me into his platoon. Warakira was a Mugandan and because he was easy to talk to, I told him my problem. I noticed a smile creep across his face and he took me to buy what I needed. I didn't hear what he said to the lady in the shop, but he sounded very embarrassed. Then she took me by the hand and showed me how to fix my problem. The Republic House housed the offices for administrative senior officers. My new job was to guard the gate. I learned that a Mugandan boy of my own age was part of the platoon. He was one of those people you just can't help noticing, not because of his loud mouth, but because he always managed to be the centre of attention.

His nickname was "Manager". He seemed to know everybody, he had money and girlfriends and he put on a suit as soon as he was off duty. He knew the place as well as the inside of his own pocket and gave me a first class tour when I got there. Guard duty proved to be profitable because for some reason a lot of civilians needed to get into the Republic House without an appointment. I came to know my commander as the most relaxed soldier – he wore civilian clothes even on duty, and he often stayed away for days. He never shouted his orders as most commanders did. He sounded like a schoolteacher giving advice. We were the ones who shouted the orders. It was great saying no to fat and wealthy men who wanted to get through the gate. Soon I was able to follow Manager's example and I bought myself a suit. Most of us were already off duty by four o'clock. Then Manager and I would count the money we had earned during the day. Most evenings we would go to a bar somewhere to have a good time in our identical suits, with enough money to catch people's attention.

My new post suited me more and more, and one day I overheard an interesting conversation between two staff members. Our afande and president Museveni decided to change the national currency and give each of us between 35 000 and 50 000 shillings to show his gratitude for our contribution to his struggle. Some rumours said Colonel Gadaffi, the Libyan leader, a close friend to Museveni, had given him the money to do this.

Soon, Manager and I stood at the canteen next to the Republic

House, filling out forms while being distracted by the man who counted up our money. Never before had I seen this kind of money, and both of us got dizzy just looking at it. I left him at the gate and ran to my uniport, a room styled like an African hut but made of iron sheets. I dug a hole and buried the money. I kept four hundred shillings in my pocket, and soon we invaded town in a frenzy, forgetting all about the "cool" image we'd been building. When we reached the shops, I felt terribly confused. I couldn't come up with a single thing to buy! Manager had no problems in that area, so I just followed his lead. He bought a bicycle, a dozen bras and underpants for his girlfriend, and other things. He didn't even know what some of it was for. I returned with a fine pair of men's shoes.

Later we went to the most expensive bar. We told everyone there that Manager was the son of the vice-president Kiseka and that I was the son of Salem Saleh. Everything was great until three half-drunk men entered. They refused to believe us. We felt humiliated and demanded an apology but they merely laughed as deeply as they could. We left, promising to return.

We were in charge when we returned with our guns and told them to kneel on the floor. We pretended to aim at their heads. The party ended when we realised someone might call the police and we rushed back to our quarters, laughing our heads off.

A Home

A WEEK OR SO WENT BY. I tried to figure out what to do with the money. I thought of my mother who didn't have a home of her own. I got a movement order, and on my way I stopped and bought ten loaves of bread because I knew I couldn't arrive empty-handed. I arrived by bus and walked the last five hundred metres. I found my mother gossiping with another woman outside her door. Without saying anything I pulled her by the arm and we went inside. This time I noticed how poor her home looked. When I handed her the bags of bread she surprised me with a big smile followed by tears. I wondered what would happen when I gave her the money. After I gave her the money I walked outside. When I returned she was holding the money to her chest as if she was scared it would fly away. She was smiling and her closed eyes were turned towards the ceiling, as if she were about to fly up to heaven.

I woke her up by asking if anyone was selling a house, or a piece of land and she grabbed my hand and kissed it before she said I was her favourite child. The following morning my mother was the first to get up. While eating breakfast she took my hand and spat in it. When I asked her why she did it she said it was for my protection.

She took me to a young man who was selling a piece of land he had inherited from his father. A small house was included in the price, as well as a banana plantation and two huge avocado trees. It was a good deal. Over the next few days my mother was completely impossible, giving me too much unwanted attention. She dragged me around showing me to everybody telling them what I had done, embarrassing me with loud praise. I decided to end it by throwing a party. She invited everybody in the area For most of the evening I sat against the wall, observing my mother doing everything she could do to keep the people happy. That was when I realised that God gives a good heart to those who have nothing to offer. Before I left I made it clear that if I found her with a man she would be chased away.

A few days later, Manager and I stood at the gate when a truck with a load of child soldiers arrived from nowhere. Suddenly the place was swarming with RPs. Without a word they grabbed us and threw us among the other children. The other passengers looked at us with big, sad eyes that seemed never to have seen the light of day. Most of the children had been taken from the north front, and when we learned we were being taken to Simba barracks to start school, Manager and I knew we didn't want to do it. Even when we ditched the truck, no one followed us.

These child soldiers seemed dead. All of them were quiet, sitting with their hands under their chins. They looked at us without blinking, and I could see many questions in their hearts. I still see their faces in my dreams, and I'm too scared to think what became of them. The pain is so strong and I don't know how to express it. I know one thing though – I miss all of them. I wonder whether I will ever see them again because I cannot return to my country. Those children only stayed for six months before returning to their units. They didn't want to stay at Simba barracks – they were dumped there to plant maize, not to study. They got tired of the job and many decided to go back to their units.

Everything went back to normal and one Friday my platoon leader, Warakira, was going to a wedding as his brother's best man. He entrusted me with his walkie-talkie and pistol, and told me to follow him to the wedding. I was in the car with a civilian driver and we followed close behind. With the walkie-talkie and the pistol I suddenly felt I was a big chief. With my gun I ordered the driver to go to my sister's address. Now I would show her landlady, the old woman, who had the final say. Unfortunately the old woman wasn't around, and Margie had lost her job. In fact she didn't have any food in the house, only biscuits on which she'd been living for a week.

I bought coal and some food. At one o'clock I remembered I had to drive Warakira home from the wedding party. Suddenly I was the same little China again, remembering all the scariest punishments I had been through in my life. I knew my hope of getting only a reprimand died when I found he had already left. I was ripped from my sleep and dragged out the door. With an RP on each side of me we marched to Warakira's office. Warakira ordered me outside and the RPs gave me twenty blows with a stick.

After the punishment I sat in front of the offices to try and forget the pain. I did not sit there for long before senior officer Ahmad Kashilingi arrived in a Mercedes Benz. I stood up straight and saluted him, but he swept the salute away with his hand. He waved me over and told me to get into his car. We drove to his home in Kololo, the richest part of town, where he had a mansion surrounded by a big fence. As we came to the gate he honked the horn, and an armed soldier saluted and opened it for us. We had lunch together and he told me that he wanted me to be his bodyguard. I almost choked on my food. The word "bodyguard" reminded me of abuse. I realised that Godfrey's assaults on me had stuck in my mind. Still, I hoped Kashilingi would be different from Godfrey. I stood up and saluted him before saying, "Yes, sir!"

Paradise

IN THE SAME YEAR, 1988, Kashilingi sent me back to the Republic House with one of his drivers to get my stuff. My heart was beating fast, and the sweat just kept on running down my face. Somehow I managed to pack and return without any fuss. Kashilingi gave me a room and most of my worries were over. A short while after having put everything in place, Kashilingi returned to my room and invited me to his house. As we walked through the house, I kept on seeing children running and crying, and I learned that most of them were his but from different wives. We had a quiet drink and soon I had come to terms with my new duty. That evening I had supper with Kashilingi's family. Afterwards he told me I would be eating at his home.

I didn't bother to know his reason for this; I just saluted him and looked forward to the nice food. I walked up to my uniport and stood there looking down at the fence that separated Kashilingi's residence from Colonel Julius Chihanda's and Brigadier David Tinyefunza's. Behind Kashilingi's house there were boys' quarters consisting of four rooms. In front of it was a parking lot. After the tour I went to my room and slept with a good feeling about my new life. I woke up in time for morning parade and got in line in my uniform. I was the only girl there. Lieutenant Patrick Kiberu told us the day's briefing, gave me an AK47 and introduced me to the soldiers.

The day started and Corporal Katumba and I escorted Kashilingi to the Republic House. Proudly I went and stood next to the Mercedes Benz with my gun resting on my left arm, and soon Kashilingi appeared. He stood on the veranda for a short while, staring at me with measuring eyes. Then he walked down, and we waited until he got into the car. We arrived at the Republic House without a word and followed Kashilingi through the main entrance and up the stairs to his office. I was so excited when I saw the soldiers' reactions when they saw senior officer and Director of Records Ahmad Kashilingi approaching. Of course, I knew all the fuss was for him, but I still felt like an important person – I could also use his power to become feared and respected.

When we arrived at Kashilingi's office, the administrative officer of his department, Chris, sat at his desk in the front room. Despite his higher rank I refused to salute him. I saw the anger in his eyes. Katumba, another guard, would teach me everything I needed to know, and told me to get a chair to sit with him outside the door, in the hallway. There we had to sit as ordinary guards until our boss would leave his office. Kashilingi left and we followed him in the car. I did not know where we were going and was afraid to ask, so I just kept my eyes open.

Finally all the mystery vaporised as I found myself in front of a restaurant, and as we sat down after Kashilingi, I was told not to be modest and to choose whatever I wanted. No escort had ever bragged to me about this and I had spoken with many soldiers. I felt like the most important escort in the world.

At around four o'clock we returned home. Kashilingi called me and I saw him standing there in civilian clothes.

He told me to get my gun, and then we drove to Kabaragara where he and his friends were going to drink. I was told to stay in the car and keep an eye on him. He sat outside the bar on the veranda with his civilian friends. I could even hear them whispering from where I was sitting. Kashilingi was the centre of their party. Kashilingi talked about how dangerous I could be, and said that if one of them insulted him I would shoot them all. After he said this I tried to judge what I would do in a situation like that and decided I would only shoot the one responsible.

I soon got tired of listening to their chitchat. I felt restless. Our leaders would forget us in their cars for hours. Some times we would fall asleep and they would beat us. Some officers cared about their bodyguards, but others treated us like dogs. I was getting bored and hungry. I remembered the bag that Kashilingi always kept near the gear leaver. When they had stopped talking about me, I slipped the bag onto my lap and opened it while staring at some invisible point as far away from it as possible.

I felt the shape of a pistol and all around it was a mess of paper notes. I stopped my search and picked up a note. Then I pushed the bag aside and went out, as if I was going to the toilet. In the shade of the car I looked at my catch, and to my joy the note was enough to buy a nice amount of chicken. I made a sign to a man who was grilling a few metres away, while showing my arms as wide apart as I could that I wanted a big piece. His kindness couldn't have been greater, as he hurried over with a leg, and quickly we made our secret exchange. I had to eat it as fast as I could but that was no problem because I chewed it up as if it had no bones. I went back to the car and sat down, satisfied. The mission was over.

The following day Katumba said my training was over and left me to do guard duty alone. Then he went to visit his friends around the building and I felt a bit sad. The problem was the immense boredom. After only a few minutes I rushed down to greet him. As we talked I suddenly remembered my gun. I had left it outside the door. I ran back and found an empty spot. I almost panicked because I knew from the battlefield I could get killed if I left it there, and the fear stopped me thinking clearly. Quickly, and discreetly, I asked Katumba what to do. He told me to talk to Chris. Chris smiled. He picked up the phone and called the RPs. They arrived in a minute and took me to the warehouse at the Republic House. They ordered me to roll in the mud until my uniform was wet. After changing into another uniform, Chris gave me my gun, looking triumphant. He understood that I craved revenge.

I left the office, carelessly dragging the AK behind me as I waited for someone to say something. Feeling dark and angry I went back to my chair filled with thoughts of cruelty and planned how to get revenge on Chris. At lunch time, a woman stopped us at the gate. Kashilingi ordered me to sit in the back seat, and I felt as if my rank had been stripped from my shoulders. We drove on, the woman sitting in front, and stopped at one of the many restaurants in Kampala. Kashilingi asked for the menu and handed it over to the woman asking what she would like. Her eyes grew larger and larger as she shifted between looking at the menu and Kashilingi. The waiter started looking at his nails while the rest of us stared at her.

"Menu," she said at last. Kashilingi looked at her, not quite understanding her, and she repeated, "I think I would like the menu." That was too much fun for one day, but it wasn't appropriate to laugh at Kashilingi's girl unless we wanted ten blows with a stick. Katumba and I started to sound like two steam engines – letting out the air through our noses. Our neighbours didn't have that problem, making waves of laughter roll through the place like the waves of the Victoria Nile.

A little confused and without getting an explanation for the sudden change of mood, she ordered something else. While all of us waited for our food, Kashilingi allowed us to get it all out of our systems. Officially we laughed at everything else in the restaurant, but we laughed even more as the woman joined in. After lunch we dropped her off at the taxi park and went back to the office. Only an hour passed and Taban, one of Kashilingi's drivers, arrived. He was on his way to the army clinic, on the first floor. One of Kashilingi's children was sick. As Taban waited for the child to return, he told me he was more than sure I soon would get the full rank of corporal. I didn't really believe him. I saw him as someone who had decided to compliment me.

He was a Kakwa, from a place near to Idi Amin's village. I was always impressed with the way he walked. He decorated himself with weapons of all sorts, a bayonet on each side of his belt, a pistol tucked into his trousers at the back, and then for some reason he had a rope hanging at his right side. He was small but he took up the space of a bull. The first thing I did when I got home was to visit Taban in his room. I asked him how he got the rank of sergeant. He told me he had been in Idi Amin's army where he was trained as a commando. I believed him and hoped one day to be as tough as he was.

Kashilingi and his family were Muslim, so when Ramadan began they had to fast, which meant they couldn't smoke, eat, or drink as long as the sun was still up. On the first day, when the sun was about to set, I sneaked into the dining room and saw the table laid with lots of different dishes of food and drinks. The downside of it all was that I couldn't have any of it because I hadn't fasted. Those who had not fasted were served regular food, while the others enjoyed the rest. I waited until Kashilingi had finished eating before I told him I also wanted to fast. He smiled and said, "Sure, why not?" Then I started Ramadan together with his family. Every day at four in the morning during Ramadan, Kashilingi's daughter, Kobusingye, would come and wake me up for *daku* – food before sunrise. By midday, my lips were dry and my eyes were getting even smaller. I understood why Kashilingi went home to get some rest at this time during Ramadan. At home Kashilingi looked at me and smiled, telling me I didn't have to fast in order to eat the good food with them.

I couldn't stop though. I was afraid his children would laugh at me. I told him I would not eat until the breaking of the day's fast. I was convinced my little lie had worked because he nodded with a satisfied face. I hurried down to the nearby shop and bought a litre of milk and a huge piece of hot loaf, which I hid in my bag until I reached my room. Pleased with my secret cache, I warmed the milk on my field stove, put sugar in it and started eating the sweet bread as if I had never eaten anything before that.

When I felt better, I started looking around the room and noticed Kashilingi standing in my doorway. In panic I hid the milk and the bread. He looked amused and I began to cry. I begged him not to tell his children. The following day I woke up early, brushed my shoes and ironed my uniform, and walked down to where I had to meet Taban. He was washing the car.

He had a bandage on one of his legs, and when I asked him why he told me he had caught a snake on its way down to his boot. It sounded so exciting that I almost wished that it had been me. Then I saw Katumba on his way out of the house for morning parade. He suggested that maybe Taban had fallen over his own two feet when he was drunk. Taban was a Muslim and a commando so I didn't think he would lie about such a thing. I sneaked into his room to see if Katumba was right. I came across some empty whisky bottles in a box, and later when I asked him, he told me they had been for his medicine.

Soon Katumba and I became good friends. He entrusted me with taking his letters to Kashilingi's daughter, Kobusingye. I wondered what Kashilingi would do if he caught me. Then Kiberu began a friendship with the other daughter, Aisha. I felt like a postal worker, taking letters for those boys every second day, but it only lasted for about a month.

One day I was having a cigarette with Regina, when Kashilingi called me to him. I stopped whistling when I saw him standing with a determined look and holding Kobusingye's hand. Slowly he took mine too and dragged us to her bedroom. He threw her pillow aside revealing all her letters, and banged our heads together. I didn't want more of this, and told him I never knew what the letters were about. Quietly he said that he was sorry for hurting me before shouting, "Don't bring any more letters into this house!" Secretly I passed the message on to Katumba and Kiberu, but they seemed determined to carry on with the girls.

Then it was time for Eid, the celebration at the end of Ramadan. Two days before the celebration the family were sent in Kashilingi's mini taxi to Rukungiri, the village where Kashillingi's parents lived. Katumba and I stayed behind with Kashilingi who still had a few more days at the office. Finally we followed the family in one of his cars, a Mercedes Benz, however we were stopped at a military roadblock because he had civilian number plates on the car. I admired the MP sergeant's red and white uniform, especially his beret. He demanded Kashilingi identify himself. I waited for his reply with excitement before he said, "I am senior officer Ahmad Kashilingi, Director of Records." The sergeant's face went limp.

When he realised what he had heard, he almost fell over when he removed the stop signs blocking the road. On our way we stopped at a restaurant. The manager appeared from his office and waitresses buzzed away from the other customers coming to welcome Kashilingi. As usual when he was in a good mood, he slapped a few of the waitresses on the bum. I nearly laughed only I was distracted by a plate of chicken placed in front of me.

When we arrived at Kashilingi's, Katumba and Kiberu put ,on music and television, while I played with Kashilingi's children. The holiday was over, and soon we were on the road going back to Kampala. When we arrived home, Kashilingi invited me to sit in the living room because he was going to play a movie for his children. Kashilingi was in a good mood, sitting in his big sofa, with a glass of beer on the table in front of him. Then he told Kobusingye to fetch me a beer too. I had never had anything to drink in front of him, so I refused at first, telling him I had never had a beer before. He insisted I drink it.

Savage Heart

THE FOLLOWING DAY, before going to the office, Kashilingi and I had breakfast together. We talked about this and that. When he asked about my parents, my hand froze. Slowly I began telling him about my father, but I couldn't finish because my tears welled up. Kashilingi breathed out heavily and told me he'd joined Idi Amin's army because his father treated him badly. I looked into his eyes without blinking and asked about his mother, but she died before he was old enough to remember her. We walked down to the car as if our destinies had made us one.

I had just been sitting outside the office for an hour when Kashilingi came out stuffing his pistol into his trousers. Katumba and I followed, and we drove to Rubiri Barracks, where we found a battalion of recruits ready for inspection. Kashilingi and senior officer Peter Karim started inspecting them and I followed. It was a poor line-up. The boys, wearing old uniforms, had their eyes on me. Kashilingi told me to choose three recruits. I was surprised by my own reaction – I felt a shockwave go through my stomach. I stood face to face with those hungry boys, confused about whom to choose because most of them had heard what Kashilingi had just said. I almost drowned looking at their sad faces, so I had to close my eyes in order to hide away. When I opened them I focused on the boy in front of me. "My name is Benoni, sir!" he replied to my question, and I told him to step out in front, flattered by his way of addressing me. But reality came crashing down when the boy next to Benoni whispered, "Take me, please, Afande!" and I couldn't resist. Later he nicknamed himself "Sharp".

I was about to pick the third one when Katumba called me over to show me a child named Jamiru. He told me that Jamiru was a Muslim and he would be a great help when we needed to slaughter Kashilingi's hens. I felt like laughing, but when I saw how young he was I asked for him.

Back at the Republic House, Kashilingi told me to call Taban, so that I could take the three boys to Mbuya in the military store, and get them some uniforms. Out of the three young soldiers, I grew fond of Sharp because he was funny, always full of jokes. He never stopped calling me "Afande China", even though he was a bit older than me. With Benoni it was entirely different. He was in his mid twenties, and for him a woman belonged in the kitchen. He was aggressive and refused to recognise my rank. He was only a recruit, which meant I was years ahead of him when it came to military experience. I was annoyed about having to use cruelty to earn his respect – to get him to say the magic word "Afande".

Jamiru was on top of the world because he and Katumba had found each other and were now brothers. Katumba seemed to be a man in constant pain, and like me, had been raised in the army. Jamiru was now learning everything he could from Katumba, and soon this little twelve-year-old child turned into an ancient warrior who thought he was the best at everything he did.

A few days had passed and I was promoted to the rank of sergeant. I couldn't believe my ears when Kashilingi appointed me Chief Escort. It was so hard to hide my excitement, but again the fear rose inside me, as I looked at the grown men who had to obey my orders. My way of walking quickly changed, and at supper Kashilingi told me he would attend the morning parade to see how I was managing. Early in the morning he arrived in full uniform and told everybody there to respect me as the new Chief Escort.

My whole body trembled as he told them to take any of their problems to me. I felt like jumping into the air but then he walked around us and told Katumba to pack his stuff and to go to the office. Katumba was going to be transferred to the north front just as Kashilingi's previous bodyguard had been transferred. All Kashilingi's bodyguards who had affairs with his daughters, or told his wife about his affairs, were sent to the north front. Many of his bodyguards were children just like me, and later I came to meet one of these bodyguards. His name was Silas. Silas was now living at the officers' mess in Kololo, near Kashilingi's home. Silas had been shot more than four times while fighting at the front, and he was getting thinner every day.

Silas was light-skinned and looked a little like me. We became friends. That day it was Katumba's turn to be sent away – I knew it could be my turn tomorrow. The very last time I ever saw Katumba he was blind. I never found out what had happened.

As chief escort I wanted to be treated with respect because there was nothing on earth I was more afraid of than being seen as a coward. I was frightened to give up. I had the rank and title to decide things about the escort, but I was also a young girl of thirteen who was afraid that the soldiers would disobey my orders. I felt desperate and it seemed that I had to do everything I could to make the men fear me.

By four o'clock in the afternoon we were back from the offices. Kashilingi hurried into the house and I followed, but waited near the living room. Soon he came out from his bedroom and told me to get Jamiru ready. When I had seen them off, I went to the kitchen where the house girl Namaganda was busy washing dishes. I stood with my hands on my hips next to my pistol and bayonet, waiting to be served. When I realised she was going to ignore me, I decided to take a plate of food from the oven. I hid my anger.

As I was about to take some food, Namaganda grabbed the plate out of my hand like an eagle catching a baby chicken. I turned and smiled before asking her the reason for this. She explained this was the only food left and she was saving it for Kashilingi's nephew, Julius. "You mean you didn't save any food for me?" I burst out, wanting to slap her. I didn't, as she was much bigger than me. I hated losing battles so I grabbed at the plate and we started pulling. Both of us let go and the plate fell to the floor. Suddenly her size didn't matter anymore, so I kicked her in the stomach. She doubled over and I walked outside. Standing a few paces from the doorway, I heard quick footsteps at my back. I turned around, and saw Namaganda approaching with a kitchen knife. "Do you want to kill me?" I asked, drawing my pistol. I remembered my bayonet, so I put away the pistol. She stood there waving the knife at me. I kicked her hand and before the knife landed on the ground I had cut her with my bayonet. I left her screaming outside and went to my room.

Later I heard a knock on the door. It was Jamiru, still in uniform. He told me Kashilingi wanted me, so I got dressed and followed him. All of them, except for the little ones, were waiting in the living room. Namaganda sat next to Kashalingi, her arm in a bandage, and I sat as far from them as I could. "Do I leave you here to terrorise my family?" he roared.

"No, Afande!" I replied and explained what had happened. "I

always tell you that this "thing" is dangerous, but you don't seem to listen (referring to me as the "thing"). One day I will find all of you dead," he said. After he spoke he let me go to bed and I fell asleep easily, pleased with his judgement.

I woke up later. Outside I met Aisha in front of the house. She was sad and when I asked why, she told me that her boyfriend, Kiberu, was being transferred to another unit. I was pleased because I didn't like him – he was a lieutenant who always prevented me from doing my duties.

Still, I pretended to be sorry. We continued our conversation until I got a chance to tell of my problem with her. I got jealous seeing Aisha's breasts bounce up and down whenever she ran, and I wished that I would grow up faster so mine would also look like that. She told me to pull my growing breasts for a couple of minutes each morning, and in a few weeks they would be just like hers. I really looked forward to the day when mine would be bouncing in the air.

I left Aisha standing there, and went inside to the breakfast table. Julius and his cousin Emanuel were having breakfast and as I joined in they told me about a party at their college. None of us were allowed to go anywhere at night – even I wasn't allowed to be near the gate after six. We decided to sneak out anyway because we knew that Kashilingi would be home late. In the evening after supper, Julius and Emanuel went to get dressed, but I was already dressed in my uniform because I wanted the boys at the party to fear me. Before we left, I told Sharp, who was on night duty, not to tell Kashilingi in case he returned before us. When we arrived, the men at the entrance let us in without having to pay.

Most of the people wanted to speak to me, and I got everything for free. Soon I was getting tired because of Julius and his cousin, who introduced me to everybody. We returned home at around five o'clock and as I was about to fall asleep Taban knocked on the door, telling me Kashilingi was calling for me. When I got to the living room, Kashilingi was in his nightgown, shouting at Julius and Emanuel. "Yes Afande!" I saluted.

"Didn't I tell you never to go out at night?" he asked. I couldn't really find the answer, but when I looked down he ordered Taban to drive the three of us to the military jail in Mbuya barracks.

In jail many of the guards didn't like me because of my proud attitude. They told me they would make me sweep and clean in and out of the jail. But I didn't care because I knew I had enough money to buy their anger. At eight o'clock the next morning, Kashilingi arrived. He told the guard commander to give me a hard job and left with Julius and Emanuel. I was hurt. I thought it wasn't fair to save the two boys and leave me behind. I wondered whether I meant anything at all to Kashilingi who left me in jail with one uniform knowing I was a girl who needed to change. As soon as Kashilingi left I stayed in the cell and watched through the window.

The guard commander approached and said that even Kashilingi wanted to punish me. He said he would make me work until I looked like a pig. After he had finished I put my hand in my pocket and showed the sergeant some money. His eyes opened wide and I said I would give it to him if he promised to let me be. That night the sergeant sent one of his comrades to buy beers and invited me for a drink. We sat on the grass watching the stars. The sergeant was now my friend, and as I was about to return to the cell, he said: "I hope Afande Kashilingi picks you up because I'm off tomorrow".

Many things crossed my mind before I lay down on the concrete floor and slept. The following day I was more than sure I would be released but after dawn I still hadn't seen Kashilingi and gave up for the day. In the evening of the third day he arrived with Jennifer and Jamiru, and when the guard commander brought me out, Kashilingi was angry when he saw my uniform was still clean. He called the guard and told him to beat me with a stick, and as I was about to lie down, I heard Jennifer say to him I had had enough. Kashilingi called off the punishment and ordered me to get into the car. When we arrived home I ran to my room where I remained until the next morning. After breakfast we drove to the office. Later Kashilingi came out and told me to call his lover, a woman who worked as secretary to Rwigyema, now a major general and the Minister for Defence. When I got there I met with Rwigyema's bodyguards. One of the boys, named Happy, was my best friend, so I began gossiping, forgetting what I had come for.

Rwigyema appeared from his office and took me by the hand saying, "I can't work to that noise!" I panicked as we stood in front of his desk. He told me to sit in his chair. "You are now the minister, so go on and sit there!" Nervously I looked at his secretary who just smiled. After a while he told me I was free to go, but he had to report the incident to

Kashilingi. I felt the pressure of the minister's promise, and without looking I slipped through the door and was back on my chair. I waited for the major general's arrival, but fortunately he never arrived and I escaped yet another punishment. Rwigyema and I became friends. Whenever he caught me making a noise with his bodyguard, he would take me by my ear and pull it until I promised never to make a noise again.

At first I admired him – when he was the senior officer I once knew in the bush, and later I came to love him for his kindness.

House of Tragedy

KASHILINGI WAS A BIG FAN OF THE THEATRE, particularly the troop led by Jimmy Katumba. He watched their plays at weekends with his daughter, Jennifer, because his wife lived in his home town. He left me in charge one weekend, saying, "Don't kill anyone, understand? Take care of them!" I stood on the veranda with Regina and Alex, an escort who had only been with us for a couple of months.

As we stood there, a civilian driver named Tumwine arrived whose job it was to drive Kashilingi's children to school. The two boys looked threateningly at each other because both were in love with Regina. A moment later they argued about where the 35th battalion had been transferred.

Tumwine asked Alex how he could be sure when he couldn't even spell his own name. Alex replied by calling Tumwine a cow. I heard a loud slap and when I turned, I saw tears in Alex's eyes, and that was it. He walked down towards his room saying: "Now I'm even being beaten by a civilian!" I went inside the house leaving Tumwine and Regina there. Shortly after having spoken to Jennifer I met Alex, who had got in using the back entrance. He was carrying an AK47 and three magazines taped together. I could see he was ready to shoot, but I had no choice. I told him to leave the house. I could hardly see his eyes as he pointed the gun at me at close range, and asked, "Do you want to die?"

Since I was the Chief Escort I felt I should take full responsibility, even if it meant sacrificing my own life. I stood there looking down the barrel, sweating. I couldn't stop begging Alex and the more I begged him the more upset he got. I thought of screaming but I was afraid. Suddenly I saw Tumwine walking slowly towards Alex and when he grabbed Alex from behind, a bullet struck the wall close to the bedroom where the children were asleep. I realised it was only the beginning.

Jennifer walked from her bedroom, and then disappeared again. I stood there confused, knowing I had to join the struggle. My main worry was the magazines, and I struggled until I managed to remove them. Now my only worry was that one bullet left inside the chamber. Suddenly I saw Regina pulling Alex's gun. I shouted, telling her to go away. But it was too late, I heard the second shot and I saw Regina fall to the floor. Blood covered the floor where she lay. I turned to Alex, and he too had been shot.

Regina's leg was badly hurt. She was bleeding more than Alex, who had been shot by the same bullet. The bullet had penetrated her thigh and the muscle had been destroyed. The house was in panic. Children were crying and everyone was looking to me for help. After having tied Regina's leg, I decided to take her to the hospital. I left Alex there. I was upset and at the time I didn't care whether he died or not.

Tumwine and I carried Regina outside, and as we were putting her in the car, Colonel Chihanda walked out of his house, stood behind his fence with his arms crossed, and asked, "Are you busy killing yourselves?"

When Regina was in the car I thought about Alex and realised I may have done the same, so I changed my mind about leaving him behind. I ordered Tumwine to drive as fast as he could and soon we arrived at Nsambya Hospital. Regina was already in a coma when I left her in the doctor's hands. Alex was hit somewhere close to his private parts, but it was not life-threatening. Tumwine and I stayed in the car and I was terrified about how Kashilingi would react to this. I thought he would transfer me to the north, but if I were lucky, he would send me to jail. A doctor came and told me Regina had lost a lot of blood and they needed someone to donate some as soon as possible, otherwise she might die. "Regina needs someone with the same blood group," he added. I stood there and looked him in the eyes because I didn't know anything about blood groups. The doctor was a kind man and explained it all to me.

We drove home with double indicators on. At home I furiously ordered all the grown-ups into the car and soon we were back at the hospital. The doctors checked our blood and of all the people I brought back with us I was the only one who had the same blood group as Regina. I was taken to a room and told to lie down on a mattress. I complained when they explained that I had to fill up the bottle at my side. After they had taken my blood, the nurse told me not to get up. I ignored her warning and as I was about to get to the car, I passed out.

On our way home, we saw Kashilingi's Mercedes Benz coming towards us at high speed. As soon as we stopped he started shouting at me, but I was still too weak to respond. I heard him ask Tumwine, "What's wrong with this one, is she also shot?" He drove very quickly to the hospital and I knew it was not over between Kashilingi and I. After some time Kashilingi returned and from my bed, I asked for a doctor even though I was okay. I told the doctor what had happened and he helped me by lying to Kashilingi, saying I needed a good rest.

I stayed home for some days, eating and relaxing, and that's how I escaped the punishment. Days later I went to visit Regina, and she told me that her leg was turning blue. That day she asked me to sleep over, and all night I watched her as she cried over her leg. The next day a doctor came to see us at home. He said Regina's leg could not be saved and that we had to call Kashilingi who was at work, to go to the hospital. At night in the living room, Kashilingi told everyone Regina's leg was to be amputated. We all laughed, despite the sadness, when Kashilingi's niece begged that Regina's leg should be given to her. When asked why, she said, "Because it has red nail polish."

Months later, Regina returned home, and spent most of her time hiding. She turned into a chain smoker, and this time she didn't hide from Kashilingi. There was hope for Regina – they wanted to send her to Germany for further treatment. Every time I returned from work she would call for me. Mostly she spoke about what future she might have. Somehow her words and tears affected me deeply, and it made me start to think about my own future. I became troubled that every day was the same, and I seemed to be losing my mind.

I hated the Republic House, though what troubled me most was that I could see no end to my misery. Everything at home seemed against me and was worse when Kashilingi ordered me to keep my door open. One day I asked Kashilingi for a transfer. He shouted at me, threatening that if I really wanted it he would send me to the north front. The man I hoped would be a father to me had turned against me, and I didn't understand him anymore. I was beginning to be frightened of him, though I hardly knew why.

Things were getting out of control and I had to come to terms with reality. The sexual abuse started the day I became his bodyguard. Kashilingi was very powerful and I was scared to think ill of him because I thought he could see what I was thinking. I saw no way out. All I did was try hard to concentrate on the good things he did.

My stomach gave me pain, but still he abused me. Whenever I cried and told him that it was painful he would say, "I will do it slowly." Every night he knocked at my door. Once I pretended to be fast asleep and in the morning he asked me why I hadn't opened the door the night before. Soon he realised my trick, and I was ordered to keep my door open. I couldn't do anything. I was powerless. I had nowhere to go and no one to talk to. I had to deal with it all by myself and I wondered if there was anybody out there who felt my pain.

There are so many things that happened to me – things I saw that I couldn't talk about. I'm afraid to face them and let it into my heart. I was like a sheep. I had to say yes all the time. My soul seemed to be owned by the afandes and I wondered if I would ever own myself again.

I could not understand Kashilingi. He abused me at night and the following day he would send me to call his girlfriends. On other days he would put me in jail. I was so frightened of him and I always will be. It feels as though he has power over me, as though he owns me.

After Kashilingi's abuse I would cry. Luckily, music was always there for me. I would lie in my bed and cry, listening to music until I fell asleep. The music seemed to feel my pain, and it always calmed me down. He knew very well how I felt because every time he abused me I would cry. He would ignore my tears.

I will never know why. I was there to protect him and he treated me like I was a machine! One day I reported myself sick and stayed in bed. I was so upset but I didn't know why. I needed to do something. I went to Kashilingi's house where Regina was alone watching television. I passed her and went to the fridge, grabbed a beer and drank it, while she stared at me, saying nothing. I walked back to my room and the next thing I remember I was shooting in the outside toilet with my AK47. Suddenly I heard Regina cry for help, so I dropped the gun and hurried to help her.

She was lying on the floor holding her leg, and when I asked what had happened she told me that she had fallen from the sofa because she heard terrifying sounds. Deep inside I cried but I could not tell her it had been my fault. Instead I convinced her it was the noise from the building going on nearby. Once again Regina was taken back to the hospital for another operation, and I was allowed to stay with her until she was discharged.

Regina was never sent to Germany. She was taken to a local doctor who made her an artificial leg. She didn't like her new leg, and most of the time she preferred the walking sticks. Regina was getting fat, and that raised many questions. One day at the office, Colonel Julius Kihanda, asked me if Regina was pregnant. I told him I hadn't thought about it but I hadn't seen her with a boy since she returned from the hospital.

He looked concerned and told me to find out. After work I hurried to Regina's bedroom and asked if Kihanda's suspicion was true. She started crying saying "It's all Kashilingi," but I could not understand her answer. I left her crying and went to do some shopping. On my way back Lieutenant-Colonel Moses Drago who lived in the neighbourhood, called me over. My entire body shivered as if I had been struck by malaria, and the few things I carried became heavy. I stood still and after having breathed like a tired cow, I managed to approach him. He was sharing a few beers on his veranda with one of his friends, Lieutenant-Colonel Peter Karamagi.

Drago asked questions, but I could not answer. My paralysed tongue refused to co-operate. Before I left he told me he was not as dangerous as people thought, and all he wanted was my friendship. I walked away feeling proud, thinking I had spoken with one of the most popular war heroes. Most of all, I was excited about the cars that he drove, colourful ones with horns that honked like animals. Now my greatest dream was to get a ride in one of them.

When I got home I was still excited, so I went to Regina. She was still sad so I offered her a cigarette. As we smoked she told me she was pregnant. I put pressure on her to tell who the father was, but she refused. A few days later, Regina gave birth to a girl. Later I heard Jennifer say the child resembled Kashilingi. Since Regina had kept her pregnancy secret, and hadn't said whom the father was, Kashilingi's daughters were desperate for the truth. One evening when everyone sat in the living room, Kashilingi asked Regina to tell us the whole story. Regina looked as if the world was about to end as we stared at her and the child in her arms.

She broke down and cried. She told us a bodyguard of Drago's had raped her one day when she was alone in the house. I knew that she was telling a lie because bodyguards were not permitted to enter a senior officer's home – there are always soldiers at the gate. Besides, she would have told me when she revealed her pregnancy. I got angry and walked away.

The next day was Saturday, and everyone slept late except for me. I went and knocked on Regina's window. I demanded that she tell me the truth otherwise I would never smoke with her again. Regina told me that Kashilingi had forced her to lie but still refused to tell me who the father was. Later that day my sister Margie and her boyfriend came to visit me. Before leaving she told me they were moving to Kabale. I was sad. However, when she told me she was expecting a baby I was pleased. I was beginning to enjoy my life because of my friendship with Drago. He made me feel safe and relaxed in a way no other man had ever done and every time I was away from him I missed his company. He spoiled me with everything and seemed to understand my worst fears and my greatest pleasures. I got to know him as a twenty-four-year-old who could only write his name. He was also a very unselfish man.

In most of the places where we went together even a private felt free to address him as a friend and not as a lieutenant-colonel. One evening, Drago and I were having an ice-cream at a café. In the middle of the conversation he interrupted, suggesting I ask Kashilingi for a transfer to his battalion. I nodded with a sad smile.

I was standing at the gate with Sharp when Drago arrived. He gave Sharp money to keep him quiet and we drove off in his Landrover. He took me to a friend's house, where we watched some movies. The movie Delta Force made me forget all about the time, and it was midnight when I returned. At the gate, Sharp told me that Kashilingi had been looking all over for me, and to my distress he hadn't been able to keep quiet.

The following day Kashilingi called for me and accused me of betraying him. This time he sent me to the "bad guys" in the cells of the Republic House. At eight o'clock in the evening I heard Drago ordering the MPs to bring me out. He spent some time with us, and before leaving, he handed some money out to each of us. Now the military police had become the "good guys", and we spent the night drinking. When Kashilingi came to release me, I didn't really want to go. I smelled heavily of alcohol, and to protect my new friends, I hardly breathed until I got home.

Because of Kashilingi's behaviour, I felt more and more desperate every day. I began to notice a side of my personality I couldn't really control. Many times I thought of running away, though I knew he could use his authority to make my life a living hell. There were many things I needed to think about, only I couldn't think straight unless I was far away from Kashilingi's reach, and I rarely got that chance.

In the morning, at the office, I told Kashilingi I needed to visit my mother. When he refused, I started crying and he changed his mind and ordered Chris to grant me a movement order. When we got home I went to Drago's. Unfortunately I was told by one of the bodyguards, Kabawo, that Drago had gone north to his unit. I returned home with Kabawo's promise to take me there the next morning. That night I went to bed without food – I was too excited. I also needed to prepare my pistol, as I knew very well that where I was going was a dangerous place. I equipped myself with five magazines and my journey began. When I arrived, Kabawo was waiting for me at the gate. He too was ready with his AK47. We walked to the bus park and boarded a bus for Lira.

When we reached Karuma Bridge, I looked down into the splashing water, trying not to remember what once happened. I was relieved when Kabawo interrupted by showing me an elephant walking at the side of the road. Soon we arrived at Dr Obote's home town, Lira, where many buildings had been bombed and most of the people were cold and poor. The few people I spoke to were rude. Most of them just stared at me and walked away, without responding. After eating, Kabawo and I came across a military truck going to Kitugum. There were many soldiers and all were desperate for transport. It was hard – everyone struggled to board the truck. There were two lieutenants, and both wanted to sit in front. Kabawo started arguing with them because he wanted me to sit there, since the truck belonged to Drago's brigade.

Drago was very happy when we arrived and he told Kabawo how much he trusted him. After we changed our clothes, Drago invited us into a restaurant. Later, the District Administrator joined us. He wanted us to join him at the dance club. When we arrived, the manager hurried to prepare a place for us and we spent most of the time talking and drinking. The next morning, Drago ordered the Brigade Administrator to slaughter some cows and give some meat to every soldier. Drago invited all his men, from the rank of sergeant and above, to his quarters, and as the soldiers began preparing the fire, we took a short trip to town. The town was poor, there was not much to see, and the shops mostly contained sugar and salt.

The only buildings still intact were those I had seen the night before, and the roads in the city offered no better comfort than those in the bush. Many of the children were naked, and most seemed not to have washed for several days, but I could see a smile on their faces as they passed me, carrying containers of water. The troubled city and its weary inhabitants made me change my mind from going any further. As we walked back to the barracks, I met my uncle Caravel who told me that he had been put under house arrest.

As we spoke, Drago stayed at a distance, and that gave Caravel a chance to question me. I told him that Drago was my friend, but he didn't believe me, and when I asked him the reason for his arrest, he chased me away. Drago seemed desperate to know how I came to know Caravel, and when I told him that he was my uncle, he invited him over. But the lieutenant who had been sent to call for Caravel returned alone. As we sat at the fire, Drago told everybody to stop calling him "Afande", and I realised that he was getting drunk. One sergeant stood in front of everyone and said that he wished all commanders were like Drago. After he had finished talking, Drago and I went into the house, and we heard them sing until morning.

While eating breakfast the next day, Drago suggested that I stay for another day. I wanted to but I had been granted only three days. After breakfast I walked down to Caravel, and as we spoke, I felt as if I would never see him again. The thought made my eyes wet, so I said goodbye. After a few minutes, Drago told me that I was to go back by military aircraft, which would be landing any minute. We said goodbye and all I could hope for was to see him again. Before Gulu we landed in the bush. There were many dead soldiers, and I couldn't believe my eyes. I saw the dead officers being sorted from the rest, and loaded into the aircraft. I cried in silence about the dead soldiers being buried in a mass grave. Every soldier there seemed tired, and I was shocked when I noticed their behaviour, acting as if they didn't know who they were anymore. Their uniforms were torn and they smelled bad.

There were so many casualties that some had to wait for another helicopter. After having unloaded the wounded at Gulu barracks, we flew to Kampala. At eight o'clock in the evening, I was in bed. What I had seen stuck in my memory, and I doubted if it would ever leave me.

I spent a long time thinking about the dead soldiers, and in the end I could not find any reason for their death. The next day at the office I noticed all those women I usually ignored. They were all looking for their sons and daughters. I spoke to one of them who had been left standing at the death office.

This tired, crying woman told me she had not seen her son for years, and that she had been coming to this office for more than a year. I knew for sure her son was dead and had been left to a miserable fate in the bush, just like many others. One thing I couldn't understand was why the authority did not tell the truth. On our way home I questioned whether the NRA would point out the graves of the comrades who had fallen so bravely in the battle belonging to one man.

Farewell

A WEEK HAD PASSED SINCE MY RETURN from the north. It was 1989, and I was standing next to Kashilingi's Mercedes Benz. I heard a car stop at the gate. It was Chris.

He stepped out and ordered me to call Kashilingi. I refused, telling him that since I was the chief bodyguard, I should know why. Chris got angry and took my refusal as a form of revenge. We stood there and argued until he told me about the fire at the Republic House. I ran and told Kashilingi and in panic we all drove there. Senior officers were everywhere, watching the Republic House in full blaze. There was tension, shock and panic in the air. Everyone was asking everyone questions.

The fire damaged the Directorate of Records and many senior officers believed the fire started in Kashilingi's office. As the Director of Records, it seemed to be up to him to have all the answers. Kashilingi had lost many of his private documents, including money from the safe.

Kashilingi was suspended, and he was troubled by this, seeing it as a betrayal. I asked myself whether Kashilingi could be behind it, and if so, why?

I remembered Kashilingi having complained about his rank to someone – I believed it was Museveni (I had heard him on the phone about a month before). I answered the call personally, and this person had asked for Kashilingi, not Afande Kashilingi. The rank issue and the way he had addressed Kashilingi made me think it was the president and the army commander.

Curious, I had listened from behind the curtains, and after the conversation, Kashilingi walked away angry. After a few hours I found no reason for him to have committed this crime, and as far as I knew, the only person who had the authority to suspend him was the president. I even thought it could have been the president behind it, since he was a man who achieved his goals, no matter what the sacrifice. I was convinced he could have decided to burn down the Republic House just to frame Kashilingi. Perhaps Museveni felt Kashilingi had become too powerful.

Kashilingi was no longer coming home late, and he wanted the gate closed twenty-four hours a day. At some time during the day he would sit in his car. It seemed to me he was hiding without knowing it. I became frightened of my life, as I had no idea what would happen. I had crazy ideas like soldiers coming in the night to kill everybody. It made me scared, and I decided to cut a hole in our fence through which I could escape if I needed to.

One morning I was still in my room when two senior officers arrived from Rubiri first division with one platoon – Bamwesigye was the brigade commander, and James Kazini his second in command. Kazini was aggressive and he seemed excited. The two senior officers ordered Kashilingi to hand over all of his uniforms and AK47. They left him his pistol. For the first time, I saw tears in Kashilingi's eyes, and I was certain that this was the end for him.

The bodyguards and I lined up in front of Kashilingi, and he was told to choose two and one driver. Jamiru, Bogere and I were staying, each with an AK47 and one full magazine. The powerful man feared by the most was now powerless. It was a big blow to me, and I had to act before it was too late. I knew that soon they would ask me questions, which I couldn't possibly answer. In the evening I asked Kashilingi to let me take my stuff to my mother, and without hesitation he agreed. Early the next morning, Jamiru and Bogere helped me pack my belongings and drove me to the bus park. I arrived at my mother's safely, but many of my things had been broken.

On the third day I returned to Kashilingi and things were never the same again. He was full of suspicion and he spent most of the nights walking outside the house. I was getting bored staying at home every day, and without Kashilingi's permission, I went to town.

There I met a mechanic, a friend of Drago's, who used to fix Kashilingi's cars. I stayed at his garage watching movies until late in the evening, when he drove me home. At the gate, Jamiru stood on guard with his gun ready. When I ordered him to open he said he had been ordered not to let me in. I tried to force him but he said if I continued he would have to shoot. I was extremely hurt and disappointed. I had protected this man for so long. I saw him as a betrayer and found no option but to get revenge.

I walked away letting Jamiru think I had given up, sneaked around the premises and used the hole in the fence to get to my room. I went straight for my gun but it had been taken away. Powerless, I sat on the floor and cried. Early in the morning I went to the gate and ordered Jamiru to call Kashilingi. Kashilingi stood at a distance and asked what I wanted. I asked him to tell me why he was doing this, and he said that I was being used to spy on him. There was nothing more for me to say, and before walking away, I said, "Afande Kashilingi, thank you for everything!" I went to Rubiri barracks to Captain James Kazini's office. They told me to return the next morning for deployment. I wondered which unit I would be put into and suddenly I imagined the officers waiting there with their drooling mouths. I was confused, and frightened, and I didn't know where to go. I decided to go to Drago's place because it was better than having to face a thousand lions. Some days later I heard that Kashilingi's home had been invaded by the military police.

When Kashilingi heard of his impending arrest he called the president, but Museveni was out of the country. Kashilingi didn't give up and called the new army chief, Mugisha Muntu, who denied any knowledge of what was happening. Kashilingi was afraid. He asked them why specifically Rubiri barracks, and not Luzira or the Military Police headquarters. When the soldiers couldn't answer he knew that if he surrendered to them, he would be slaughtered. Kashilingi stood in front of the armed soldiers with his briefcase begging them to let him drive alone to the army chief's office. The soldiers stuck to their orders until Colonel Julius Kihanda came along and convinced them to indulge Kashilingi. Kashilingi was allowed to drive his Mercedes Benz, closely followed by the soldiers, and when he arrived at the offices, he locked his car and walked inside while the soldiers guarded the place.

Two hours passed, and the army chief happened to be on his way to lunch. When he saw the building surrounded, he asked, "What are you doing here? Am I under arrest?"

"No, sir, we're waiting for Afande Kashilingi to leave your office." When the chief realised Kashilingi had been missing for two hours, he panicked. Radio calls were made to all units of Uganda to be on stand-by, and the chief ordered a raid at Kashilingi's.

A few days later I met one of Kashilingi's daughters who said the raid had been unforgettable. The military police who'd been sent there to watch the children's every move, turned nasty and had emptied the house. They kept the children at home – they couldn't go to school, and the house was turned into a military barracks. The children were put under house arrest, and they could only look through the window as they prayed for their lives to be spared. Since the house belonged to the Ministry of Defence, Kashilingi's children were kicked out and in a matter of days they were out on the streets.

I was sad to hear about what had happened, and I couldn't understand why these children were treated like enemies. But I didn't have any energy to feel sympathy for Kashilingi's children because things were also going badly for me. Intelligence staff hunted me, and all of them were asking the same questions. "Why did you stay behind? To spy for him?" These men accused me of being Kashilingi's niece. Perhaps they thought I was guilty as Kashilingi.

In my heart I knew they were aware I was not Kashillingi's niece, but they were trying to scare me with blackmail. I was harassed almost every day. They would only leave me alone if I gave them sexual favours. I refused to give in, fighting hard to keep up my spirit. During that time I met Colonel Julius Chihanda on foot and in civilian clothes. Surprised, I approached him and he told me he'd been suspended for helping Kashilingi.

When I told him about my situation he told me to back off before he got into more trouble. People I had counted on for help avoided me. I came to understand when I heard that Kashilingi's childhood friend, a captain who had been suspected of helping him to escape, had been tortured and beaten to death. The most shocking news was that a dear friend of mine, Kashilingi's younger brother, Byarugaba, had been hacked to pieces in his Rukungiri home. I knew I had to do something to avoid the same fate.

One day Drago arrived, and the following day we drove to his new brigade in Anaka, near Gulu. When we arrived, he ordered his bodyguards to make a fire. We sat and talked about Kashilingi. Drago himself didn't think that Kashilingi was responsible, though he couldn't understand why he had run away. The next day the brigade was moved next to Idi Amin's birthplace. Koboko was a small town, close to the Sudanese border.

The next night Major Bunyenyezi and his brigade joined us. Sudan was also in the process of a military build-up on its border on the other side of the valley. A few days later, more brigades were brought in, and I witnessed a gigantic standoff. The only good thing about it was a higher salary, and I was impressed to see privates having chicken for breakfast. Both sides had huge numbers of soldiers – there seemed no end to the lines of artillery. When the battle was called off, many soldiers seemed more disappointed than relieved because of their lost income.

Drago's brigade was sent to a different battle somewhere in the Gulu bush. I was sent to his house at Gulu barracks. After several days of doing nothing the division commander, Colonel Peter Karim, called me and asked if I knew where Kashilingi was. He assured me that no matter where I went I would have to answer for Kashilingi. I could only look him in his eyes, salute him and shake my head. He let me go, troubled and tired of questions, and I wondered whether there was a place where I would be safe.

Weeks later Karim went to Kampala, leaving Colonel Stanley Muhangi in charge. I was inside the house, ironing my uniform, when a soldier walked in and told me Afande Muhangi was calling. I was afraid of what he wanted from me. I told the boy to tell Muhangi I would be there after doing my ironing. A few minutes passed before a lieutenant appeared at the door ordering me to go with him. Surprised, I told him I had to take a shower first, and he insisted on waiting until I was ready. Muhangi was waiting behind his fence and as I was about to reach the gate I heard a helicopter. When I looked back at the fence there was no Muhangi. It landed right in front of me. Drago climbed out and walked passed me, right into Muhangi's house. Relieved, I went back to the house. I couldn't have felt happier than when I heard Muhangi had died of AIDS a few months later, but I still couldn't help asking myself of how many female soldiers he had killed this way.

A few days later I returned with Drago to the front line. Since we took power in 1986 Drago kept on fighting, always being transferred from one unit to another, always to another battlefield. In Gulu we were always walking, hunting for rebels. But Drago wasn't the only one who kept on fighting. Many of my fellow child soldiers continued to fight and they too were now as hard as Drago. The difference was they were lower ranked-soldiers and were forgotten.

Many of my fellow child soldiers were orphans. Their families were killed in the Luwero bush war, and since there was no one left to miss them or find them, they were left to fight the war until the end. Anyone who got shot or got their legs and arms cut off was sent to Mubende Casualty Wing. When Mubende was over-crowded with casualties, the government got rid of them – they were just left to steal and live on the streets. Most of them were killed. Many Acholi were considered rebels, and even if some of us knew they weren't, we still saw them like that.

The hate we felt for Obote, the former Ugandan president, never changed, and the Acholi seemed to pay the price. Drago's second in command spoke Kinyankole and he took everything that happened very personally. To him every Acholi was a rebel, and they deserved only death. Every time we captured an Acholi we had to kill them and Drago hated this. Drago was a tough and hardened soldier except when it came to civilians. Then he wanted to keep his hands clean. Unfortunately, some of the leaders saw it in another light.

Most of the interagency officers were one tribe and those who were not were always watched. Our brigade interagency officer spoke the same language as Drago's second in command. This made Drago change things. One day, Drago returned from the State House where he had gone to attend the army counsel with President Museveni, and when he arrived, there were Acholi men who were tied up in the most painful way, Kandoya style – tying the arms behind the back at the elbows until the chest is pulled apart.

Some had died and others were in a terrible state because they had been beaten with their arms tied behind their backs. They weren't wearing any shirts and you could see their chests about to pull apart. They were on their knees, without any words to say, their eyes begging for mercy. But we turned and looked away.

I tried to ask God to turn me into a general so I could save them, though my wish never came true. The terrible thing was that every time you showed sympathy for the enemy, you were accused of being on their side. The best way was to hate them, although inside you knew you did not. Drago went berserk, fighting the second in command. After the fight the major went to Kampala.

Drago was later transferred to Karamoja in the east. Looking back on everything, I know that only a few of my comrades survived. Many died on the battlefield, of AIDS and in front of the firing squad. Others took their own lives. The good officers died in car accidents, in ambushes, from AIDS and of heart attacks.

To try and forget them I would take a cigarette and smoke. All had fought hard to save their country and they had survived so much only to die later on peaceful ground. With tears and sadness I search for them in the sky, hoping that one day I might see their faces again. With all of this happening we couldn't find anyone to talk to about our fear because the person next to you was going through the same thing.

You had to keep your fear and die with it. In the evening we lined up for hours under orders from our unit political commissar who told us how to dedicate ourselves heart and soul to our leaders. We were told that civilians didn't know anything and we couldn't trust them – anything that took place in the army should remain in the army. It was a crime for a soldier to talk to a journalist or to tell a civilian anything. However, the journalists from our newspaper called *The New Vision* were allowed in our barracks, only they reported the opposite of the truth.

Time passed and something strange happened. Drago began to annoy me, not only what he said, but his clothes and the way he ate his food. Everything disturbed me. He tried to give me as much care as he could, but it all meant nothing. I packed my things and left without saying goodbye.

Living with Injustice

I WENT TO THE MILITARY POLICE in Kampala and was relieved to hear that Major Kaka was the commandant. He was a special friend of mine and a good man whom I had known since the NRA had been a group of rebels. One of the guards took me to Kaka's office, and before I could salute him he shook my hand.

We chatted and I told him I wished to join the military police. Without giving it a second thought, he grabbed the phone, called the Directorate of Records and ordered my transfer. Everything went faster than I could have hoped for, and soon I was on my way to my new quarters, escorted by the administrating officer of the unit. After unpacking my stuff I returned to Kaka and we went to a restaurant. He asked me if I was a Rwandese, and I kept silent with fear. I knew answering such a question could be crucial – I couldn't work out why he wanted to know. Kaka's smile remained, and after lunch he took me to a bar.

At the morning parade Kaka didn't show up and the second in command informed us that he had disappeared with most of his body-guards. I was crushed by the news. It had to be a bad sign. Just when I thought I'd found the right place, the most important person there abandoned me. Once more everything seemed to go in the wrong direction. Weeks later, when nothing more had gone wrong, I found I enjoyed my new job. There was nothing I loved more than my new look with my red beret and my belt with red and white stripes. I looked very smart in my military uniform.

I loved my new look, but others hated it. Soldiers and civilians hated us and they called us names like "Kanywa Omusayi", meaning "drinkers of blood". There was nothing on earth people feared more than being jailed at Military Police Headquarters. If you were brought to MPHQ, you might never leave. I came to love the military police because MP officers were too scared to abuse me. If they had, I too might treat them badly if they ended up jailed at MPHQ.

I took my job and my rank very seriously, and soon I earned the respect of most of my colleagues.

One of my colleagues whom I can't forget, was Sarah. She was only half black, and many soldiers called her a half-caste. She was older than me and drove a green Mercedes Benz for Afande Doctor Ronald Baata, who worked at the Republic House as Minister of Health. Sarah too looked very smart in her military uniform. She was a very beautiful girl. When Dr Baata got another driver, things went bad for Sarah. I later learned she was staying with Captain Jafali. Sarah died while having an abortion – like so many other girls who were with us.

One morning, at the parade, Afande Biraro, the acting military police commandant, told us that Major General Fred Rwigyema had died in the battle of Rwanda, and a shockwave of surprise and sadness ran through the lines. That same morning I also heard the reason for Kaka's disappearance. We were told he was doing a fine job in Rwanda along with half the Tutsi soldiers from the Ugandan army who had chosen to start a new life in their motherland, Rwanda. Rwigyema's sudden death made me think of my two uncles, Caravel and his young brother M.M.

I couldn't help swearing at Kaka, blaming him for not telling me who he really was at the restaurant when he asked where I was from. I'd lost my opportunity to go with them, but I had to find a way of establishing contact and at least hear their last words before it was too late. I was wandering in town one day when I met Happy, a friend of mine, who had been one of Rwigyema's bodyguards. I had written a letter to my uncles and he showed me to a shop where a woman took my letter and told me to return in a week.

Then I found out that Caravel had died in battle. M.M. was now my only hope, and I tried to convince myself that he would survive. I was so anxious that every time I thought of writing, the fear of getting bad news stopped me. I was getting depressed and was angry with myself for not writing to him. I felt lost without anybody to talk to, and I began to feel like a spare part that is easily replaced. I found it hard to look at myself in the mirror. I felt I'd become ugly.

My stomach had begun to grow in the strangest way, and sometimes I wished never to have been born. I carried on my duties despite everything – driving around town with soldiers, checking movement orders, and soon other people began to comment on how I looked. I often felt the comments were mild insults, but one day an officer managed to make me laugh by suggesting that I was pregnant. I got hungrier than ever, and I couldn't stand anything but grilled chicken and I threw up whenever I couldn't afford it. I had slept with Drago and had fallen pregnant.

One day after work I was lying on my bed. Suddenly I felt a kicking sensation from inside my stomach. I thought I might have a parasite growing inside me because I blankly refused the possibility that I could be pregnant. The next morning I went to the doctor who instructed me to take six months' leave. The doctor said I was pregnant. I couldn't understand how a soldier could have a human being in their stomach.

My stomach continued to grow with no intention of stopping. Finally I forced myself to believe I was pregnant and nodded whenever people asked. Going on leave forced me to find another place to stay and Drago found a place for me at his friend, Musa. Drago was happy and told me that if it was a girl I could have her but if it were a boy he would get all his names.

Some weeks later, Margie came to me with a letter from Helen who was dying of AIDS at my father's farm. In the letter she told me how much she loved me and that her greatest fear was to die without my promise of being at her funeral. She told me to be strong, hoping I wouldn't be too affected by her death.

I couldn't speak as I folded up the letter. I felt I was dying inside. It was too much for me to comprehend that I decided not to think about it any further. Margie and I argued when I told her I couldn't go. I was hurt by what she said, but she too had been hurt.

Two days before Margie left, she told me she would never see me again. But I knew she would forgive me eventually. A few depressing days passed and I went to the hospital for an examination.

The doctor's surprise showed in his eyes as he examined me. Now he looked busy and as he backed away to the door he told me to stay put. He returned with nurses who took me by the arms, and slowly we walked to the labour ward. I sat on the bed, amused by those women who acted as if they had been possessed. All of them were much older than me. I couldn't feel a thing, though they told me I was about to give birth. I couldn't work out how the baby was going to come out of me. "Are these woman crying from excitement, or are they simply letting the whole world know that they are having a baby?"

A white doctor examined me. He told the doctors who were standing by that I wouldn't be able to push out the child and they had to help me give birth. The moment came when I too started crying, and soon I had removed all my clothes. I jumped all over the place trying to escape the pain, but it just wouldn't stop. Now I realised I was the weakest woman there because they still had their clothes on and stayed in their beds. I bit my fingers, and pinched my body, though it did nothing.

I decided to stop giving birth and went towards the stairs, but just as I was on my way out of the labour ward, a group of doctors and nurses grabbed me. At around eleven o'clock at night, on 3 March 1991, I gave birth to my son. The difference between me and so many other women soldiers was that my child was born with a father who was ready to take responsibility for us and not discard us. I had seen so many women with more than three children and no clothes for them.

I blamed the NRA. Now I had a child whom I loved more than anything else. I realised these women felt the same. Most of us were too young to be mothers, but in the NRA there were no limits on anything because of your age. It was a crime for a child soldier to say, "I cannot do this because I'm a child." Too many young mothers had to work out how to be both mothers and fathers.

The next morning Drago and his family were all over the place, and I could see life in Drago's eyes as he struggled to hold the child in his arms. Later that day, my son and I were driven back to Musa's home, which was crowded with people who had been invited to the party. It meant nothing to me. I was thinking of Helen and my family. I left everything to the happy people and went to sleep. I loved my son so much, and whenever he cried, I would cry too. He gave me hope and strength and whenever I was sad, I would look at his face and smile.

My leave was over and when I returned to my unit, I began to see other women very differently. I approached a girl not much older than me. This lance corporal had two small children. She looked at my son for a moment before looking at the one resting in her own arms and said, "I can only guess who their father is." No one had asked these girls whether they were ready to be mothers, nor did any of these officers intend to take responsibility for their children.

At the morning parades there was a moment of silence when the commandant and officers walked towards us, and you could hear babies and small children crying for their mothers who were on parade. None of these officers seemed to hear the cries of their own blood. Soon every sound was drowned by our singing voices. Our happy faces would convince most people. Our faces were those of children, but our bones were stronger than iron.

A caring look would make us shy away, afraid to reveal our weakening sorrow. Most passers-by would only hear our voices and see guns in the air. They would call it life, and wish to join in, not seeing what lived beneath our actions. The artillery unit at Bombo barracks was taken over to make space for a "women's wing" in the Ugandan army. It looked as though somebody was trying to forget what had been happening by sweeping all these mothers away under the same carpet, like something you want to dispose of quickly.

Perhaps they intended to help us, though we wondered why all this hadn't been prevented in the first place. I didn't think putting so many broken souls together would solve anything. I imagined, from my own experience, all the women blaming one another more than their abusers. Nothing changed and I was convinced the women soldiers in the NRA were nothing but Museveni's treats for the hungry lions in command. Soon the women's wing was overcrowded and many were forced to leave the army with the ridiculous amount of five hundred dollars and an iron roof. These five hundred dollars seemed to be too much for the women to handle, and it was decided they would receive the money in two payments. And since the NRA had not given them any land, they would probably have sold their iron roofs the moment they became civilians. Five hundred dollars only provided food and rent for two months for a mother with two children.

Many of my child comrades were also sent away from the army because many of them went mad. They would shoot other soldiers before turning the gun on themselves. Many of them died this way, and not one of our leaders cared, although it was happening right in front of them. I was one of the fortunate mothers in the NRA because my child's father, although busy, cared about his child.

Spirits Behind the Curtain

We will never enjoy this world, and we will never see what others see even though we walk the same road.

I WAS DISAPPOINTED TO FIND Lieutenant-Colonel James Kazini to be our new commanding officer. Kazini had no respect for life, and you could see the thirst for blood in his eyes.

The chief before Kaka, senior officer Silver Odweyo, had been thrown out of office to stand in line on death row at Ruzira prison. That's where he died after having been reported for treason by Kazini, the then second in command of Rubiri barracks. James Kazini claimed that Odweyo was going to get radio codes by bribing a radio operator.

Odweyo was one of the many officers who served under Obote's regime, and was therefore easy to frame. He denied all allegations but Museveni seemed, as always, to be easily convinced by Kazini. Kazini had changed the military police, including almost stripping the prisoners of their rights. The prisoners' health was in a state of emergency. Still, Kazini kept prisoners away from the hospitals.

The jails were cold and Kazini made prisoners, except for senior officers, sleep on the concrete floor without blankets. They were often left with only their underwear and very bad food. When I added everything up I began to think he was the cause of many prisoners losing their sight. Many prisoners must have been very ill because many of them also had blood in their urine.

Kazini's treatment of the prisoners made me open my eyes. I began to see the horrors of these jails where many soldiers suffered for a long time, even before he had all the power. I learned that many prisoners had no idea of why they were being kept there, and most had been there for some years without trial. I knew many of these soldiers from the battlefield and in my eyes they were heroes who had fought hard to be free. Now they had to beg for cigarettes. Many prisoners died because of the torture, James Kazini's favourite game. He tortured soldiers with his bodyguard, Corporal Kinyata, who eventually became his second in command. Kinyata was a young, uneducated boy and he was extremely brutal to those he didn't like. He controlled the entire unit in the name of his boss, and he even had the power to beat and torture Kazini's junior officers.

Kinyata wasn't a big problem for me, but the new regimental sergeant major wanted to have a sexual relationship with me and when I refused he removed me from my old room to share one with another female corporal. When I got a nanny to help me take care of my son, the room became too small for four people and it became hard to breathe at night. My son's health was my major concern and I began harassing my lower-ranked room mate as I hoped that she would succeed where I hadn't and be assigned to new quarters. The sergeant major didn't give up. He kept on watching for any mistake I made. One day, after I had eaten, I forgot to put on my beret again. He called me over and asked about my beret. I touched my head and realised that I wasn't wearing it. He called a sergeant and ordered him to roll me in the mud. After that I was given seven days extra duty. I was ordered not to leave my post and I couldn't even try to because he kept on checking on me. I stood there and looked at my military uniform getting wet from the milk of my breast. I thought about shooting the sergeant major and his family, but my love for my son prevented me from doing it.

I had just returned one afternoon and was breast-feeding my son, when Drago suddenly appeared. When he saw the room overcrowded with beds and guns he was angry, blaming me for not telling him. I was surprised to see him so concerned. I hadn't bothered to tell him, I thought people would laugh at my problems. Drago wanted me to go and stay with a friend of his, Senior Officer Peter Karamagi, who had a big house outside the city. Before leaving Drago gave me some money and told me to buy some furniture. The very next day I dumped my stuff on the back of the truck and left with my son and our nanny.

The house had five large rooms apart from a shower, toilet and a kitchen. Behind the house were the bodyguards' quarters where I felt free to go whenever I got bored. One of the bodyguards was a Mugandan boy, Tim, whom Karamagi had taken under his wing. He lived in one of the rooms at the bodyguard quarters and soon we became friends. Tim had lived in this house even before Karamagi so he knew the area well, especially where all the voodoo men lived.

I desperately wanted the rank of officer, so on one of my very first days there, Tim escorted me to one of the voodoo men. The garden was overcrowded with children, and I was surprised to see only two women. We went inside and met the voodoo man. With big ceremonial gestures, he introduced himself as Muwanga. I was invited into a dark and creepy bungalow. The first thing he told me to do was put my money on top of a cow skin. Before he began to tell me of what had brought me there, he spat on the money.

I heard a strange sound and a movement from behind a curtain. He told me there were spirits behind the curtain telling him to give me three different kinds of medicine. I had to burn the first medicine and sniff the smoke it gave off. The second medicine I had to mix with my bath water. He held his breath for a short while before he continued. The last medicine was to be hung in a tree in front of the house at exactly six o'clock in the evening – without anybody seeing me.

I was about to tell him the difficulties of the last task, when he warned me that any complaint would destroy everything. Before six o'clock I was in front of the house watching to see if anyone would see me at my strange task. I started to climb the tree as stealthily as I could holding a small bag of medicine between my teeth. Suddenly a twig snapped under my foot and I opened my mouth in alarm. The medicine dropped to the ground, so I had to climb back down and search for it. I knew most people had spotted me so I pretended to have lost my watch. Just after six o'clock, the medicine was hanging far above the ground. The bathing task was easy, but when I was about to burn the first medicine, I was embarrassed to let anybody see what I was doing. I closed the window and almost suffocated in my room.

The next morning the bag had vanished from the tree. I was sure I would get my promotion within weeks. I was utterly desperate for more rank, as it would help me escape the sexual abuse of our administrative and other officers.

It's hard for me to confront my past because the more I look at it the more pain I feel.

Three weeks passed without any sign of the promise I had been given, and soon I was back at Muwanga's door. After we talked he left me alone for a minute. I couldn't wait to see the spirits. I looked at the curtain, drew it aside and our eyes met. The dog was huge – it seemed to have been there for centuries. It only looked at me for a second before it decided to ignore me and laid its head on its paw. I was angry. I wanted my money back – plus more for the embarrassment he caused me. Because I was in the military police Muwanga complied without hesitation.

One day Kazini called me into his office and showed me a signed letter. He asked me whether the signature was Kashilingi's. Knowing this man could be up to anything, I told him I didn't know. He looked me in the eyes and said I was lying to protect my uncle. Kazini knew very well that Kashillingi was not my uncle, but Kazini was always like this. Many who knew him said he smoked a lot of drugs and he could change his mind at any time and said things that were hard to understand.

The signature was Kashilingi's. I was afraid to tell Kazini the truth because he might claim I also knew where Kashilingi was hiding. Before I left he told me Kashilingi had been arrested. What I realised was that now I had become one of his targets. I left scared and anxious, hoping he would soon forget about me.

The next day just after lunch I was standing at the MP compound. The sergeant who stood a few metres from me was reading the government-owned newspaper *New Vision*. When he looked at me I instantly felt that something was not right, so I walked over to him. He stopped reading and hid the paper behind his back. Then he showed me the headline. "Kashilingi arrested" it said.

Soon after I had seen the newspaper a convoy of military cars packed with armed personnel drove in. The cars were driving so fast I didn't see if it really was Kashilingi and I still had some hope that it wasn't. I was afraid because I knew that if Kashilingi was arrested then I too might be arrested. Soldiers were ordered to be on standby. Suddenly everyone started running up and down and it seemed as though Idi Amin had been arrested. I couldn't do anything. I remained standing where I was because I didn't know where I belonged. Soon cars full of senior officers started driving in one by one and I got really frightened as everything started to look like an execution. Most of the soldiers were looking at me and wanted to know how I felt about the arrest.

Their questions made me more nervous and I thought of hiding, but that would only have been like hiding in the lion's mouth. Instead

I sneaked out to see Kashilingi who was surrounded by all the senior officers. He was handcuffed – both his legs and his arms. He had no shoes on and was wearing what looked like something he wore for sleeping. It seemed he had been ripped from his bed in the middle of the night.

Even though Kashilingi had done bad things to me I cried without knowing why when I thought he was going to die. I ran to the toilet to hide. A few minutes later Kazini called for me. I stood bravely in front of the senior officers and watched as they made fun of Kashilingi. One of the senior officers asked me why I never left with Kashilingi. When I couldn't answer he told Kazini to keep an eye on me, to make sure I didn't help Kashilingi escape.

They ordered me to look Kashilingi in the eyes and tell him he was stupid to run away. I couldn't see the end, as the pressure increased. When I cried, one of them told me not to cry for a man who had betrayed the NRA. After his humiliation, Kashilingi was placed in a tiny cell without windows from which he couldn't possibly escape. They kept him handcuffed anyway.

The only time I saw Kashilingi was whenever it was my turn as orderly sergeant and I was responsible for all procedures to be carried out in the barracks. A couple of weeks later a prisoner came to me and showed me a letter he had hidden in his pants. It was from Kashilingi. At first I could only hide it behind my belt, and hurry to a safer place. The letter was addressed to Major General Salim Saleh, and it instructed me to deliver it. I didn't know if I could trust this prisoner. He could have shown the letter to Kazini hoping to get himself pardoned.

I wasn't much use on duty that night, so I prepared to deliver the letter to Saleh, a close friend of Kashilingi's. I believed Saleh to be the same breed of war heroes as Kashilingi. Early in the morning I went home. After breast-feeding my son, I joined Karamagi's girlfriend in the living room. I waited until she had finished her breakfast, then showed her the letter, telling her I had to deliver it the very same day. After calming me down she convinced me that I should deliver the letter.

Some days after the incident one of the military police officers called me to his house. He wanted to know if I was capable of helping Kashilingi to escape. Some of the officers hadn't thought so. Kazini told them he was going to trick me to see how I felt about Kashilingi. Then the call came from Kazini. He asked me if I wanted to visit Kashilingi. I replied saying "Afande, I hate Kashilingi since he betrayed the NRA. I have nothing to do with him, sir." I saluted. Kazini remained seated in his office chair and started to swing from side to side, with his hands flat on the table.

I stood perfectly still, watching the light skin on his face. His eyes got smaller and smaller, just like a cobra about to spit. He then called for Lieutenant Ruhinda and when I heard the sound of a large bunch of keys, I knew Ruhinda was on his way. Ruhinda was tall and skinny, with a long nose hanging on his long face. If you weren't in one of his cells he would be a true friend to you. When he appeared, Kazini ordered him to take me to Kashilingi, unlock his cell and let Kashilingi and I talk in peace.

At first I was too surprised by Kazini's persistence but it was an order, so I obeyed. The distance from Kazini's office to the cell quarters didn't give me much time to think. As soon as Ruhinda entered the cell quarters I ran off and stayed in town the rest of that day. Kazini's behaviour made me think he was a sick man trying to gain more rank by creating a scenario where he personally could prevent Kashilingi's escape. A few days later Kazini moved me out of Kampala to Karuma Bridge, where the military police had its only detachment. When the administrative officer told me I went straight to Kazini's office with my son, but he wouldn't let me talk and ordered me to leave.

Karuma was still considered a dangerous place, not only because of the rebels but also because of the dense population of tsetse flies and mosquitoes in the area. Kazini knew that very well but didn't give a damn about my son or me. James Kazini was eventually rewarded for his deeds. Within a year or two he managed to move from captain to major general, while those who were senior to him still have the same rank today.

After a few months in Karuma I heard that Kazini had been promoted and sent to Gulu to be a 4th Division Commander. Kazini left his bodyguard, Corporal Kinyata, in the military police. This was a shock. Kazini knew perfectly well that everyone in the military police hated Kinyata, but he left him behind anyway. Kinyata was harassed every day by everyone there. I don't know what happened to him.

Kazini is now a major-general and commander of the army.

Separate Worlds

MY SON WAS ABOUT NINE MONTHS OLD, and because I didn't want to leave him with Drago's family, I took him to my sister Margie. I told Margie what was happening and she said she would keep my son, only her husband didn't want him because he was so young. So Margie took me to a home for children, and there we met a woman who said she would keep him. When we got back to Margie's house her husband had changed his mind about keeping little Moses. The following day I went to Karuma happier and feeling a little stronger.

The road from Karuma to Pakwach ran through a national park where the rebels had one of their strongholds. Every morning we would wait at the roadblock for civilian vehicles to arrive. Our job was to escort civilians who were mostly going to Arua. I loved Karuma, not because of its rebels but because we had a good commander. I had a good time with my fellow sergeants, and later, Stephen felt like a brother to me. Stephen and I did convoy work together. I desperately wanted to tell him of my troubled life, but I couldn't because I knew that a friend could easily turn out to be an enemy.

Our job was dangerous – it had already taken many lives. Every morning my friends and I would eat half a chicken each before we left because we knew any day could be our last. I eventually didn't care anymore whether I died or not, but thoughts of my son made me try to dodge the bullets. The convoy work was hard and it required a lot of skill to control the civilians who only seemed worried about time, and seemed to forget the danger around them. The convoy was extremely slow because of the trucks, and other drivers with fast cars became impatient. Every day we beat civilians who broke the convoy because they put everyone at risk and we hated that kind of disrespect. Many comrades lost their lives on this route trying to protect civilian lives. Whenever they questioned our rule we would be furious. I was probably one of the angriest soldiers, believing that a beating was the only solution. Some would even stay away when they knew I had the shift.

Our priority when putting a convoy together was to minimise the danger of casualties in an ambush. The trucks would be in front, then private cars in the middle, followed by the large buses. One morning, just before we left, a young soldier of around twelve years old came to me. I was too busy to pay him any attention though he kept following me around as I ordered the soldiers aboard. That day we were ambushed and the boy was killed, spilling his precious blood on my uniform. I hated myself for not listening and I cried and cried because I couldn't bring him back. I tried to work out what the boy had wanted to tell me, but I never got my answer.

I was greatly affected by his death – I thought about my own death almost every day. So I went to the commander and asked him to grant me a few weeks off from convoy duty. Now my job was to make sure that the soldiers in Karuma did their duty, including those at the two roadblocks guarding both sides of the bridge. In the detachment there were only two girls, and I was the only sergeant there, outranking the corporals who were all a lot older than me. I had to be as hard as a rock to do my work. One evening, when I went to the roadblock a private told me the guard commander had left his post. I went to the centre of the village where I found the corporal drinking. When I ordered him out he threatened to shoot me, and in front of everyone he told me to kneel down and beg.

As I knelt down his girlfriend started to laugh at me, and I could see in his eyes that if I didn't do as he said I would be killed. After begging him for some time he let me go – his biggest mistake. Ready to explode, I went back to the roadblock and ordered two privates to join him, steal his gun and bring him to me. The privates returned and said they hadn't managed because the corporal had his gun over his shoulder. It was getting late and before returning to the camp, I ordered the soldiers to be ready with the corporal the following morning. I couldn't sleep that night. I tossed and turned in my bed thinking of this lower ranked "thing" who'd humiliated me in front of a group of civilians. I badly wanted revenge. Very early in the morning the two privates brought me the corporal. I took him to the parade and ordered him to lay himself face down in front of the parade. He was surrounded by several soldiers holding sticks – fresh from the bush. They whipped him until they'd used up ten of them.

A few days after the incident when I was sitting at the roadblock, a white, four-wheel-drive pickup arrived. The driver was a white man, and as the soldiers checked his car, he walked over to me and introduced himself. His name was Paul. I said who I was and he invited me for a drink. He told me he was an American working as part of the World Food Program in Kenya. Paul was tall with long hair, which made him look tough. He was curious about what had made me join the army but I couldn't say because it was a serious offence to discuss anything concerning army life with a white man. Paul wanted to know if I was happy with my life. I said yes, and smiled. I tried to change the conversation by asking him if he had any children. He still asked questions and more questions – they were getting too sensitive, so I told him I had to go. Before I left he asked me if I could meet him in Gulu at the Acholi Inn. I saw that this man might be my opportunity to get a better life, and I was sure that nothing was impossible for a white man.

I ran to the detachment commander and told him I had received a message from Drago who wanted me in Gulu at once, and without hesitating he granted me the day off. I went back to the roadblock and got a lift. I was soon standing in front of reception at the hotel.

The receptionist looked at my uniform and refused to have any such person in the hotel. Luckily he showed up before I lost my temper. He was surprised to see me in my uniform and suggested he buy me some clothes in town. Soon we were back at the hotel's restaurant, which seemed like another world. Everything seemed to be so ordered, from the way the tables were set out to the way one was supposed to eat. When I looked around, everyone sat with straight backs, looking as though they were ready to leave at any moment. They looked as though they were at a ceremony, eating their meals in slow motion with knives and forks. I ignored them and decided to use my hands as any normal person would.

When I looked at Paul he smiled and asked me to try out the knife and fork, but I gave up when the third piece of meat escaped off the end of it. We went back to the bar and he started questioning me again. He wanted to know everything – my age, all about army life and when I had joined the NRA. He was mostly concerned with my rank because it didn't match my age. In his country, he told me, a sergeant would be around thirty-five years old. I was forbidden to answer his questions so I lied with all my answers. Paul said he wanted to see me again, and asked me to wait for him at the roadblock. He said he would pass through it on his way from Sudan to Kenya.

Paul left for Sudan and I returned to Karuma. I spent most of my time thinking about him. I really looked forward to seeing him again. My hope of being saved by him had vanished because of his questions – I didn't trust him. However, I still wanted him as a friend. I could forget everything else except the day on which he would return. By seven o'clock that morning I was already at the roadblock. He arrived with so many presents. I had body and face creams, a five-in-one torch and a huge package filled with biscuits. He told me he was going back to America and he had no idea when he was coming back.

I was in tears after Paul drove away. I regretted everything and wished I had told him about my miserable life. Soon I was back at the convoy and the first morning there were a lot of old trucks. One of the drivers had a problem with his vehicle. I walked over to the driver and asked him to stay and get ready for the next day's convoy. He refused, saying he only had a minor problem. I put the slow truck at the end of the convoy.

Six soldiers, one armed with an RPG, went with me on that truck, while Sergeant Stephen commanded the front. When we were in the middle of the danger zone, the driver stopped and I saw him trying to fix something beneath the truck. We had no means of communication at the convoy, which made it difficult for me to stop Stephen. I fired my gun into the air, but the convoy kept on moving. The pressure was mounting because I couldn't risk losing any of my soldiers. The driver was extremely slow and I was getting angry. I ordered the soldiers to beat him until he got his truck to move. We drove for a while until we came to the hill where I was relieved to see the rest of the convoy waiting for us at the foot of the hill.

Suddenly the driver began to panic, crying out "I'm dead, I've got no brakes!" The truck was now out of control. In front of us were many buses filled with people. I knew that if I didn't give my own life those people would be squashed to death or blown up by the RPG. With my gun swinging in my other hand, I grabbed the truck's side mirror and told my soldiers to stay in the truck. The soldiers and I tried to make as much noise as we could but because of the distance between us, the other soldiers couldn't hear us.

Once more I decided to shoot into the air but it was too late. My greatest wish was to make Stephen move the convoy so we would have enough space to slow down. When we got closer to the convoy the driver wanted to jump out. To make him stay I put my gun to his neck and told him not to jump or I would shoot him. I wanted to jump out too but I knew if I survived and the others died, I would face heavy punishment. The driver was so scared. All he did was cry. He made me see the difference between being a civilian and a soldier, and how brave I had been.

Stephen realised we were in trouble but he couldn't do anything. He could only stand and watch us go to our death. At that moment I didn't know what to wish for or say to my son who was so far away. I could see my own death, and with tears I ordered the driver to swerve into the bush. He did exactly as I ordered. I don't remember how we survived the ordeal. I only remember standing in the middle of the road looking at the boy's smashed skull and broken body.

Then I saw the civilians with their hands in their pockets, looking at him as if he didn't matter at all. I thought these civilians were responsible for his death, and I desperately wanted to kill them all. Luckily one of the drivers had taken my gun away from me. I demanded it back, but Stephen told Ramadan to keep it away from me. Then I tore a branch off a nearby tree and began to beat every civilian I could reach, as I cried like a child. I collapsed on the ground and the next thing I remember was my comrades carrying me back to our camp. I had injured my right knee with the shot I fired after my warning shot. The wound was deep and my blood just gushed out. I thought I would lose my leg just as Regina had done. I thought this was the end for me. I was put on a mattress behind the Landrover and driven to the hospital about 10 kilometres away from our camp.

A doctor named Odongo gave me a painful injection in the wound. Then he started stitching me up without cleaning the wound. I complained. He said if I thought it was so important, I could do it myself. It felt as if he had done it with his eyes closed. When I told him to stop, he told my fellow comrades to hold me.

After the doctor had finished stitching me up he told the soldiers to take me to the hospital bed where my leg was strung up. In the evening the pain was worse. Soon Odongo appeared at my bedside. He wanted to give me another injection, but I refused, as I feared that he would have given me an overdose. I was suspicious because of the way he had treated me – with no respect for my future health. He was also a Lango, one of Obote's tribe. During the bush war we had been warned never to trust a northerner.

The next morning two soldiers arrived. I was very happy to see them because I needed to be taken to the toilet which was outside the hospital. The soldiers stayed for a while and I had a good time as they took me around in a wheelchair. In the evening they returned to camp and once again I was left alone. I had to hold my leg straight with one of my hands, making it impossible to move the chair around. That night it took me an hour to reach the toilet. When I finally got there I didn't need it anymore, so I lay down next to the toilet and laughed.

I got tired of the hospital where everything smelled or tasted of medicine, and I badly wanted to leave. The next time the soldiers arrived I persuaded them to smuggle me out. I was dumped in the back of the Landrover and soon I was back at camp where I was welcomed by a crowd of soldier's wives who saluted me with their high-pitched rhythmic voices. The commander invited me to his quarters, and later my fellow sergeants gave a party to welcome me home. We spent the rest of that evening drinking, and everyone seemed happy I hadn't lost my leg.

The next day I was given permission to go to Kampala to get further treatment. It took me about half an hour to get to the roadblock. There I got a bus driven by Ramadan, who had prevented me from shooting the civilians. I stayed at Karamagi for a week before going to the company whose driver had the accident. There I met the manager of the company. I showed him my knee after having told him about the accident. He told me to wait because he wanted the driver to be there. The driver had to take responsibility for the accident and had to pay me compensation for my injury.

The driver was still in a bad way, and I could see he had no chance of paying any money. I saw him as the one responsible for the accident though I decided to put pressure on the manager until he gave me what I had come for. I was paid with a cheque, and for the first time in my life I cashed a cheque in a bank.

I smiled to myself on my way home, thinking about the three hundred dollars in my pocket. I decided not to waste them on grilled chicken. I sat in the living room for hours thinking of what kind of business I could start. A few days later, I returned to Karuma, working as a roadblock commander.

My new position gave me the opportunity to meet various businessmen who often didn't pay their taxes. These men tried to befriend me by offering me money to let their trucks through the roadblock without checking their goods. Soon I became so business-minded that whenever I was off duty I would go to Gulu, near the Sudanese border, and buy powdered milk from the Sudanese refugees to sell in Kampala. I'm not sure if it was a crime to buy or sell this milk, but it had been brought specifically for refugees living in Sudan. The milk prices in Kampala changed all the time. Sometimes you would get a good price and sometimes not. You could also buy fish oil, from America, from the refugees.

Soon one of my friends in the military police bought a share of my business, but it didn't take long before I lost all our money. I thought of telling him what had happened but I didn't know how he would react so I kept on telling him business was booming. Every time I lied I bit my tongue. I even tried to convince myself that everything was okay.

I was still trying to recover from my loss when a Frenchman introduced me to his friend, Gasparot, from Switzerland. Gasparot had a company dealing in coffee and sunflower seeds. He had an African girlfriend and a wife back in Switzerland. Although I hated her, I had to pretend to love her because she knew Major General Salem Saleh. Later, Gasparot established another office in Arua that bought coffee and sunflower seeds direct from the farmers.

Gasparot and I became good friends and I tried to help him as much as I could by making sure his trucks were not checked at the roadblocks. Months later he seemed tired of bribing me and suggested giving me a thousand dollars, which he wanted me to use for business. After having signed an "I owe you" he told me it wasn't just a gift – he wanted me to pay him back later. It felt like a difficult deal though it was hard for me to give the money back with it already in my hands.

Besides, I was desperate to buy a watch I had seen in town. I went to town with my cash and by the time I got home I had already used half the money. I couldn't believe what I had just done.

One day I got a terrible headache. It was so bad that Drago admitted me to a private clinic. He got so scared seeing me like that, that he persuaded me to bring our son for him to look after. I lay in a hospital bed with a drip for three days. After two weeks in Kampala I returned to Karuma, where I made a deal with an officer in charge of the detachment. He allowed me to go to Arua, where I met my Swiss friend. He invited me to the hotel room he shared with his African girlfriend.

After a few beers I told Gasparot I had to leave – he insisted I stayed, promising to cover all the costs. At around eight o'clock the hotel got very busy and the Arua brigade commander, Lieutenant-Colonel Katagara, arrived. Since I was in uniform I stood up and saluted him, although he didn't return my salute. He had known me as Kashilingi's bodyguard. I knew him well from a massacre he had carried out near Karamoja. He drank his beer standing up and I noticed he was staring at me.

Fortunately I didn't have to be humble and I certainly did not have to run away. Once again I thanked Afande Kaka for having slipped me into the military police. Then Katagara called me over and whispered to me. He wanted me to go with him to his quarters. When I said no, he suddenly turned everything upside down. "What are you doing here with a white man? Are you spying?" I smiled and asked him what he was doing there. Katagara was irritated by my reply, and before he left he told me that sooner or later I would have to answer the question. After Katagara had left I became afraid. I heard what he'd said as the threat of a coward.

In the hotel room, Gasparot and his girlfriend insisted I smoke one of their cigarettes. While the two of them smoked, they started laughing at me. I thought they were drunk. Suddenly everything in the room started to move in front of me, even the two of them. I thought I could shake it off but everything around me was rushing at me – I thought I was going mad. Their faces had grown and it was worse every time they laughed. Then I began to laugh and couldn't stop.

My eyes felt as though they were growing bigger and bigger. Then my mouth seemed to grow too. I was tired so the two of them said I should lie on their bed. I was afraid I really was going crazy. At last they told me I had smoked some marijuana. I laughed with relief but promised this would be the last time. I had really loved and trusted Gasparot. I felt betrayed and I no longer respected him.

The next morning I left without saying goodbye. In town I was told that people in Lira were desperately in need of food and were buying anything. I hurried to a broker who told me that in a matter of days he would be ready with dried corn. Now all my money was in corn, and everything was ready to be transported. However, in my eagerness I had forgotten to save money for hiring a truck. I needed to be in Lira as soon as possible before the corn prices fell. I hurried to Gasparot's offices where I met his friend, his French partner.

Outside the office were trucks. The Frenchman owned many of them. I told him how I desperately needed transport to Lira, but I also made it clear to him I could not afford to pay. The Frenchman said his driver wanted to buy sunflowers in Lira and he'd give me transport if I would help him to buy sunflowers. He said my Swiss friend wouldn't mind if I helped him. He gave the driver some money – for the sun-flowers – and they loaded my corn.

Many customers were already waiting as we arrived in Lira, and in a matter of minutes, I had sold the whole cargo. Tired but satisfied, I checked into a hotel, leaving the job of finding the sunflowers to the driver. He returned later and told me there were no sunflowers in Lira. The profit from the sunflowers was supposed to cover transport costs.

I didn't have any intention of paying the transport costs. While try-ing to come up with a plan, the driver suggested we go to the district of Mbale where he believed we could make money taking goods to Kampala. That money could then pay for the diesel the truck had used. It sounded like a good idea to me, so I agreed. In Mbale no one need-ed to have goods taken anywhere. We drove to Kampala with an empty truck and decided to let the driver go to my Swiss friend's stores on his own.

After a day or two in Kampala I met a man in his late fifties, a cof-fee dealer who didn't have enough money to go into business on his own. He told me how coffee could make you rich overnight. I was very excited when he told me that.

He seemed honest and I trusted him with all my money. Besides feeling he was honest, I knew that many other people had also trusted him. The old man was the only one who knew where the coffee was and could not tell any of us even if he was threatened with death. Before he left, he showed us a store where we would meet when he returned. He promised to return within two weeks.

I reported myself sick so I could return to Karuma to meet the old man. A week had passed since he'd left. Every time I thought of the money I would make, I couldn't eat anything. Two weeks and a day had passed without any sign of the old man. I contacted the other "shareholders", but nobody knew where he lived. All I could do was pray.

A few more days passed and I went to the stores. The old man and the coffee had arrived the day before. I was too embarrassed to look him in the eye because of the bad names I had been calling him while he had been away. The coffee price was still high when we sold it all. The old man suggested we make one more investment, but I didn't want to risk any more money, so I took my cash and bought a minibus. A week later I saw that my bus was a mess. As soon as they had finished with one problem they would find another. I was in big trouble.

I had to return to Karuma when my money ran out. The bus repairs had eaten up all my money. In Karuma I discovered that our commander had been waiting for me. Shortly after my arrival he called for the radio operator. He was ordered to read me the message he had received from Lieutenant-Colonel Katagara. "All units stand by. Look out for Sergeant China of the military police. During her stay in Koboko she disarmed bodyguards belonging to the Sudanese rebel leader, Colonel John Garang. It is still not known where the weapons are. Lieutenant-Colonel Katagara demands that she hand the guns over or be arrested."

"Will my life end this way?" I asked myself. When I looked at the detachment commander, I could see he believed in my innocence. But his words were not as powerful as Katagara's, and I knew that I could not defend myself because of my rank.

I didn't hesitate about what to do. I asked the commander to grant me permission to go to military police headquarters and explain why Katagara was after me. The commander gave me the go-ahead. As I left he said, "I hope you win because I don't want to lose you, sergeant."

In my heart I was sure I would return to Karuma but I didn't know when or how. When I arrived in Kampala I decided to go to my Swiss friend, Gasparot. He invited me to his house with a warm welcome. He waited until I sat down and then he pulled up a chair and sat right in front of me. I looked into his eyes and saw that he wasn't the person I had once known. His face was pale, and when I told him I didn't have the three thousand dollars, his face turned red. He wanted the money he had lent me, plus the money for the truck. I was frightened because I had no money and he needed it now or tomorrow. The money I was left with was in the bus I had bought. I thought of giving him the bus but I changed my mind because I didn't know my next move. With his girlfriend sitting next to him, he told me I must not forget that she knew Major General Salem Saleh.

Because they were my friends I had told them everything. It was only then I realised the mistake I had made in telling them about the land I'd bought for my mother. He wanted it for his African girlfriend. He ordered me to stay in the house and said that if I left he would punish me. Now I was under house arrest. I could do nothing because I had no gun. I sat in one spot until it was getting dark. Everyone had been told not to speak to me, even the gardener and the house girl had been told to ignore me.

The next day we started on our journey and no matter how much I begged them on the three-hundred kilometre journey, I couldn't get them to feel sorry for my mother. I wasn't really hurt by the way my Swiss "friend" was treating me, but his girlfriend's attitude hurt me deeply. After all, she understood the ways of our people and the pain it would cause my mother and I to lose that land.

When we got there my mother seemed very happy to see us. She ran over to hug the Swiss man. I'm not even sure if she remembered to greet me before she hurried to call the neighbours. When she returned there was an old man with her.

Mother left us with her neighbour and prepared some food. She sensed I was in trouble, though I pretended to be free of worry. My mother's neighbour was a funny looking man, and while I sat alone, in pain, the Swiss man and the girl were taking snapshots of him. Soon it was time to show them around. As we walked, the girlfriend said the land was too small and she didn't like the surroundings, although she knew the land was big enough for ranching. I took her hand and begged her to accept my offer but she refused, telling me to talk to her boyfriend. I couldn't look him in the eye. I felt weak. I stood with my head down when they told mother.

When my mother realised that they were not going to accept our offer, she started crying and I cried too when she begged them to forgive me. I was the only child who could support her. I knew that I would have to find some other way of repaying them, and I had to leave my mother once more. We were forced apart again and I feared that this time it would be forever. I was right.

False Start

ON THE DRIVE BACK TO KAMPALA I suggested Gasparot take my salary until I had paid him back. He just hit the steering wheel with both hands and told me to shut up – unless I wanted to go to jail. I was really hurt by what he'd said.

At midnight I arrived at Karamagi's. Lying in bed I remembered Paul. Now I was only thinking of America. Early in the morning I went to talk to a boy who had just returned from Italy. After I told him my troubles he told me that all I needed was a passport with a fake name. He got the application forms and we filled them out together. Name of bearer, Kyomujuni, meaning "Innocent". Occupation – secretary. I had to bribe my way to the district administrator's office and again I bribed the secretary to put my forms on top of the pile. Then I went to the passport office where I had to bribe two more officials to prevent my passport from getting stuck there for months.

Everything needed money so I decided to sell the bus. The engine was in bad condition and I couldn't bear to fix it anymore. I had run out of patience. I sold it for a thousand dollars and nearly all of it went on the passport. When I left Karamagi's home everything seemed to cost a great deal. I moved in with a family I had known through Kashilingi, and since I lived there for free I had to buy the food.

A few days later I received my passport. All I needed was a visa. I knew some Baganda boys who were ready to help me except they had no money. I was taken to Babumba, manager of a team going to the 9th Special Olympic Games of 1995. Babumba and I had met at the Republic House, and when I asked him to help me he looked as if he just burned his fingers. He told me he could not risk his life by helping a soldier to get an American visa. "Oh, you mean my sister who worked at the Republic House?" I said. Fortunately he believed me, and said the visa would cost me nine hundred and twenty dollars. I looked down before asking him if he could lower the price. With a smile he told me his office was not Owino (one of the biggest market squares in Kampala at that time).

I left my passport in his care and promised to return very soon with the money. I walked all over Kampala that day and all the people I had once helped would not help me. Everybody told a different story. I was getting tired and hungry and as I was about to give up, I met Justine's husband, Ronald. When I told him about my trouble, he suggested I sell him my mother's precious land. He had the money ready and there was nothing else I could do. I began to cry as we walked up the stairs to his lawyer.

I was so confused that I did whatever I was told. This time, however, it was different. I felt wounded for life. I went back to Babumba, paid him and thought this was all I needed to go to America. When I returned home they told me Kashilingi was going to be taken to court. At eight o'clock in the morning we went there. Kashilingi was standing in front of us. I could see he was desperate for his freedom. He had spent nearly four years in jail and this was the first time he would appear in court.

A few of his friends and a few journalists from *New Vision* were there. I didn't think the government would give him a fair trial. At first Kashilingi was being charged with treason and later as a deserter. The government claimed he had been captured on the battlefield fighting with the rebel group called the Allied Democratic Forces (ADF). In court, Kashilingi insisted he had been kidnapped from his hotel in the Republic of Zaire, now the DRC. He said his friend, Major Kyakabale, who had been a Brigade Commander in Kasese, had arranged the kidnapping.

Shortly after Kashilingi's arrest, Kyakabale had been promoted to the rank of lieutenant-colonel. He too was sent to prison for some very obscure reasons.

Kashilingi's case lasted for two days before he was released. All of his riches were gone and his name was forgotten. A few days after Kashilingi's release, I left the family I had been living with and went to live with one of my cousins near the military police barracks.

I didn't tell her that I was on the run – it was too dangerous for her to know. Besides, I feared that she might get frightened and chase me away. I told her of my plans to leave the country though she didn't believe me. I guess she thought I was too troubled to be capable of such a move. On my way to check on my visa I met Stephen whom I hadn't seen for some time. He wanted to know about the business, and I told him that I had bought a brand new minibus that had just arrived at Mombasa in Kenya. I felt really bad lying to him. All I hoped for was that some day I might make it up to him.

Babumba told me the visa had been granted. The problem was the Olympic team was arriving at Entebbe International Airport and I was worried about security agents there. I told him to give me my passport. I decided to find my way on my own.

As I walked home I remembered I couldn't travel without a ticket and I didn't have the money. I had sold the land – what more could I sell? I decided to go to my father though I didn't know what I was going to do there. On the bus I met a woman, a friend of Margie's. She told me she had met Margie. Margie had told her that Grace, my other sister, was dead. I looked at her and smiled. Then she said, "Grace died in Rwanda." She told me the Hutu had come to her home, killed her little daughter and then her husband. Grace was taken to the road. They killed her and tied her to a tree. She was found with a sign on her saying "Anyone who doesn't know what a Tutsi looks like. Here is one."

When I got to my father, I found he was very ill. He had divorced his wife and my stepsisters and brothers were no longer going to school. The children wanted us to go to their mother who rented two rooms, ten minutes' walk from my father's. My father was alone and he hadn't eaten for days. I decided to cook for him before leaving. My stepmother tried to make out that she had been a good person and my father the evil one. But I refused to blame my father for everything.

She had no money and she wanted her children back at school but she could not sell the cows. She was beating around the bush and it annoyed me. I said to her, "Just say what you want me to do." She told me to sell three cows and to give her the money – it sounded as though she had control over us. I was hurt to see that my father with his large family was dying alone, with no one at his side. Everything my father had owned was vanishing. I think it all went into my stepmother's stomach.

I knew I was going away, though I didn't know if it was to the grave or to another life. There was so much I wanted to tell her before I left, but I couldn't because I was still afraid of her. I asked her to go with us to our father and she agreed. When father heard her voice, he struggled to get out of the bed and when he couldn't he called for me. He asked us all to listen to what he had to say. "Baby, I'm so sorry, but it was never me. I married this woman and now I have lost all of you. You are the only child I love, and if I die, everything is yours." Suddenly he stood up and said, "Don't give anything to them – they are not my children!" Again he relaxed. "But I regret one thing…" He looked at me and stopped talking.

My stepmother went mad, as though the bees had stung her, and before she could attack him, I stopped her. My father went inside again. I regret to this day that I listened. He confused me and left me in suspense. His actions throughout my childhood were never consistent with his words. He remains a mystery to me.

My stepmother and I agreed to sell three of his cows without his consent. After my stepmother left, the children and I went for a short walk. Since I knew I was going away, I needed to say goodbye to my old friends and enemies. We went from house to house. The last house was where Rehema had lived. She wasn't there anymore.

I said a silent goodbye to my friends and family. At around ten o'clock we returned to my father and I sat at my father's side, but he was in a deep sleep. I looked at his face until I had memorised every detail. I went to the children's room and watched them play. They were too innocent to see their shaky future.

Early in the morning we went to the farm. My grandmother was now blind, though she still knew me by touch. "How is he? Is my son dying?" she asked like an innocent child. "No, he will be all right, but he wants to go to the hospital. I have come to sell some cows," I answered. "Greet him from me," she said before going back inside.

The cows were grazing in the field. When three of the cows had been loaded onto the truck I said we needed a fourth – the children refused and suddenly I felt ashamed. We sold the cows to one of our neighbour's boys and I put the money in my pocket. We went to a hotel where I told them to eat whatever they desired and while they were eating, I planned my next move.

Finally I told them I had changed my mind about giving the money to their mother. I asked them if they had passport photos. They said they were at home. "I want you to listen carefully. Go home and get the photos so I can open an account for you." I told them where we should meet. When they were about to leave I felt broken inside, so I called them back and gave each of them some money. When they were out of my sight I hurried to the bus park and left for Kampala. The money I had was still not enough, so I hid in the bus and continued to Arua.

There I went to a Muslim family. I had once helped this man and his children at Karuma. He had run out of petrol and had no money so I borrowed it for him. He was one of the few people I trusted to help me. On the fifth day, he gave me twenty dollars. I thought of Drago but I loved him too much and feared he would be like everyone else. I was more desperate than ever.

The three month visa was going to expire and I had only eleven days in which to get to the United States. On the tenth day I told my cousin's house girl to take the children to buy two hens. My cousin was still at work. I took her largest bag and put her small television into it. I was about to leave when I realised I could fit her neighbour's television in the bag as well. I struggled to get to the mini taxi with both television sets on my shoulder.

I was close to panic when no one wanted to buy black and white television sets. I thought of returning them though I didn't think anyone would understand why I had stolen them. I managed to sell them for fifteen dollars to a man who fixed radios. The money was enough to buy a ticket but since I was going through Kenya, I needed money for transport. I was panic stricken because I had nine days before my visa expired.

I went to a Ugandan travel agent and paid for the ticket, however, the man there told me I would have to get it in Kenya where they had another office. That day I went to where Drago and his girlfriend, Rita, had a shop, but he wasn't there. Rita was there but we had never become friends.

Drago had left my son in Rita's care. I had come to say goodbye to my son who wasn't there. I felt deep pain but as always I couldn't show any weakness or pain in front of anyone. I sat at her desk and looked into her eyes. Then I said, "I'm going away. Please look after my son until I return." She didn't say a word – she just kept her eyes on me until I had left.

Outside I met Drago's brother, Eric. I told him I wanted to see Drago and he told me he had left Drago at a wedding. The word "wedding" made me see the state of my life. I tried to imagine where I was going and it seemed as if I was moving slowly into never-ending darkness.

Again I begged from people I had helped in the past and I got money for transport. The next day I went to the mini taxi park and got onto a minibus travelling to Busia, on the Ugandan-Kenyan border. On the taxi I met two civilian boys whom I knew from before and they promised to help me get over the border.

I had nothing but the clothes I was wearing and some photos of me and my friends in uniform. I was very frightened. One thing I promised myself was that I wouldn't be captured. I was prepared to die rather than be captured. At the border I showed them my passport. The man there looked at me before asking why I hadn't used Entebbe International Airport. I didn't know what to say and kept quiet. He stamped my passport, instructing me to go and wait on the other side where the Internal Security Organisation (ISO) had their offices. Many of these security men knew me, and my heart began to thump in my chest. There was a policeman at the border gate, which made me feel safe – no policemen knew me.

My friend didn't know what to do. It was all up to me to solve. Suddenly I saw a ladies' room on the other side of the security office. I thought that toilet would either save or kill me.

I went into the toilet and stayed there for a while. When I came out I went straight to the border gate. I managed to walk through the gate without a problem. When I felt my feet on Kenyan soil I sat down and thanked everyone. My friends could only look at me and shake their heads. We then boarded a bus and early the next morning we arrived in Nairobi. Kenya was very different from Uganda and it was as though I had come from the jungle. Everyone seemed busy, rushing around. There were cars hooting and buzzing everywhere. I was overwhelmed even though my friends were holding my hand.

Together we walked to the travel agent where I had to pick up my ticket. There a man asked for my passport and I gave it to him. He then told me that the American Embassy had asked all travel agents to send people who would be travelling to America to the American Embassy before issuing them tickets. I didn't think it would be a problem, and on 2 August 1995, I went to the American Embassy in Nairobi. My visa's expiry date was 9 August 1995. I went through the gate and when I got to a small barred window I stood with my passport in my hands. A woman came to me and took it, looked at it and gave it back to me, saying I must wait for another person.

A man came up to me. He also took my passport and checked it and then said the games had already begun. "What else are you going to do in America?" he asked. He told me he would have to cancel the visa. When he grabbed a stamp I shouted at him to stop. I took out my photos and movement orders from the envelope and began to cry. I looked at the man who was about to reject me. I gave it all to him and as he looked through the photos I cried, begging him to help me. When he looked at the photos a second time, I explained everything. Finally he said he was sorry and cancelled my visa.

The barred window made it difficult for me to put out my hand to touch him. He had stamped my passport twice. Then he walked away, leaving me in tears. When I looked at the visa page, I saw "Cancelled without prejudice, American embassy, Nairobi" stamped there.

Everything became dark and I couldn't get my mind to work. I walked to where the two boys were waiting for me and told them my visa had been cancelled. We went back to the travel agency. When I asked them to refund the ticket they told me they couldn't. If I wanted the money, they said, I had to go back to Uganda where I had bought it.

For the first time in my life I told someone how I felt. I told the boys I was going to throw myself in front of a car. "I'm not wanted in this world, so why should I live?" I said. They looked at me. One of them reminded me of how much I had endured. Then he asked me why a "commando" like me would go and kill herself because of a cancelled visa. He didn't understand why I wanted to commit suicide, although he did show he at least thought I had a reason to live.

The boys went their way and like a mad person I found my way to a hotel. I ordered some food to make them leave me alone and tried to gather my thoughts. "China!" The voice was behind me. I turned and I saw Boxer, a soldier I had known at the Republic House.

I will never be able to describe how I felt at the moment when I heard his voice. I was all alone in a foreign country and suddenly an angel had come to me from nowhere. I told him everything and he made it clear we couldn't do anything without money.

Boxer was now a different person. He drank everything from homemade liquor to beers, and when he found me he was very drunk. He and I walked all over town talking about our experiences. He told me Kenya was a dangerous place to be because the External Security Organisation (ESO) had offices there. In the evening, I went back to

Uganda. I decided it didn't matter how I died.

The next day, very early in the morning, I went back to the travel agent. They refunded me my one thousand dollars and I went to the buses where I stayed until it was time to drive back to Kenya. At the border I handed my passport to a man who started questioning me. He wanted to know why I had returned and why I was going back so quickly. He was very surprised. When I told him I had forgotten some money he demanded to see it, so I showed it to him. After counting it he took one hundred dollars and said I would be allowed into Kenya. When I arrived in Kenya, Boxer was waiting for me, and as we walked I asked him to take me to a cheaper hotel. After paying for my room he suggested we buy a fake passport so I could go to England.

Boxer was very good at dealing in fakes and he knew all the tricks. All I did was to walk behind him like a lost sheep. He took me to a studio and someone took photos of me. We went to a place where there were people sewing on machines – many of them greeted him although he only spoke to one of them. Then Boxer came to me and asked for a hundred dollars. We went back to my hotel and there I got to see the passport. I guessed the passport had been stolen from a Malawian citizen. The woman was 37 years old and had dark eyes.

After having read it I looked at Boxer, saying anyone could see that I wasn't 37 years old and besides I have brown eyes. He laughed, saying I shouldn't think about it. I thought everything was a mess, so I asked him to take it back and bring me my money, but he refused. "It doesn't work that way," he said. This time he said he would find the right passport and gave him another hundred dollars. He came back an hour later with a South African passport. This woman had blue eyes, and when I told Boxer, he looked into my eyes saying he didn't know I had blue eyes. I asked him if he had another idea besides a passport. "Yes, you can go to South Africa on your own passport."

It sounded like a good idea, although I realised I'd used up almost half the money. Boxer told me I could get to South Africa by road. He promised me if I helped with money to get to South Africa he would make sure I got there safely. I felt I had no choice but to take this last chance. I gave him money to get us bus tickets. Boxer had already sold his Ugandan passport, so I gave him a hundred dollars to buy himself another one.

We left Kenya on 4 August 1995 for Tanzania. We arrived late that night and spent the night in Dar-es-Salaam, the capital city. Early the next morning we boarded a bus for the Zambian-Tanzanian border. We got there in the evening.

On August 7 we arrived in Lusaka, Zambia. There we took a bus to Zimbabwe, and we arrived at the border early in the morning the next day. The bus rushed through the country and finally, on the following day we left for South Africa. The immigration workers were surprised to see we had travelled through all these countries.

Fortunately, they were happy to meet Ugandans because of our country's support in the peoples' fight against apartheid. They only asked us one question: "Why are you here, and for how long?" I told them it would only be for a couple of weeks and they stamped it with "Temporary Residence Permit" and "Valid until 1995-08-23". At around nine that morning we boarded a minibus and arrived in Johannesburg at four in the afternoon. The moment I stepped out of the bus I began to freeze and looking around I saw only African people.

Boxer and I stopped a taxi, and asked the man to find us a cheap hotel. He drove us to the Chelsea Hotel in Hillbrow. At the reception I paid a hundred rand for both of us. The room was very cold. I walked back again and asked for more blankets. The man at reception was called Raja. He was from Mauritius and he was curious about where I came from. I was running out of money and told Boxer I could only support him for two more days, as we had agreed. Boxer began to cry and told me I was like his mother. He was in his thirties. I could see he was destroying himself with too much marijuana and I was overwhelmed by pity so I decided we would stay together until all my money was used up. I couldn't afford to buy food for both of us so Boxer found an even cheaper hotel, but I stayed at the Chelsea.

Every morning Boxer came to see me and I offered him my breakfast. A cup of tea and an egg was enough for me. The second day we went to Home Affairs where I met Tinus Van Jaarsveld. I handed over everything I had shown them at the American Embassy. He reacted positively to this, and with a smile he called his colleague to come and help this rebel. Boxer also had a photo of himself in which he looked just like Rambo carrying a large machine gun. They photocopied our photos, and gave us a three-month permit to stay in the country. The man then told us he didn't find jobs or houses for people like us, we had to find our own way once we had a permit to stay. I didn't care. I was happy to have escaped my pursuers.

Boxer said we should look for the Red Cross. When we got there I explained my situation to the woman there and told her I was pregnant. She gave me the address of a place called The Woman's Shelter.

It was a huge room with a cement floor crowded with all sorts of people. I was angry. I was shocked I had been sent to a place full of drinkers, drug addicts and insane people. I felt the woman at the Red Cross was comparing me to them. I didn't look down on them but I was afraid that if I stepped inside I would be lost forever.

I went back to the hotel and counted my money. I had only fifty dollars left – shelter for five more days. It was a fine morning with sunny weather. I sat outside in front the hotel thinking about how to solve the problem. The man next to me was holding a pistol and I was sure he wasn't a cop or a soldier. I was afraid to see this civilian with a gun. It would never have been allowed where I came from and I believed there were good reasons for those laws.

Then a woman in her late twenties walked towards us and stopped next to my table. She wore a very provoking miniskirt, which I had never seen before. Before I could get her attention a man had approached her. I heard her ask him: "Have you come for business?" Then he took her hand and they went inside. I was curious and wanted to know what the girl was selling. At the reception I asked a young white boy who laughed and asked where I was from. I felt stupid and, walking into the lift, a middle-aged man placed his hand on my shoulder.

Before I could speak he invited me into his office. He introduced himself as Morocka. I nearly collapsed when he told me he owned the hotel. I saw a speck of hope. We spoke for a while and I explained the difficult situation Boxer and I were in. When he had finished his whisky he called the boy from reception. He told him that from now on, both of us could live and eat at the hotel for free. I didn't know how to thank him and when I was about to kneel before him, he reached out the palm of his hands, and said: "No, don't do that!" Morocka left his office and I watched him get into his white BMW. A few days later we were hired.

I worked as a barmaid while Boxer worked as part of security for the hotel. The bar was divided into two parts. Downstairs was just a regular bar while the one I worked in was called the Sex Shop. At one end there was a porno shop with movies and all sorts of weird objects, and at the other was a topless bar with a big screen showing porno movies. I was paralysed, and for the first couple of days I didn't speak. They expected me to work topless, but fortunately Raja said I could be bar-helper and I didn't have to do it.

Dee, who worked topless and as a stripper, was an angel. She really cared about me. After work she always asked me out when she went out with Ryan, her boyfriend. We went to cinemas and restaurants, and wherever we went she paid for me. She earned a lot more than I did. She got R180 a week while I earned R50 a week. Dee's room was next to mine at the Chelsea and her door was always open for me.

Nicole also worked at the hotel but she was not like Dee. She earned as much money as Dee did, but she seemed to love money more than herself. She had a boyfriend but she still sold herself to customers who came to watch her strip shows. One evening after work Nicole invited some of us to her birthday party. When we had finished eating cake, Nicole gave me her keys and told me to get her a bottle of whisky. I left them drinking and went to sleep.

Early the next morning Raja shouted at me to open the door. He rushed in with one of the guards. I was shocked when he accused me of stealing Nicole's R50. I started crying, not because I was being accused but because of how humiliated I felt. I showed Raja my salary he had paid me the day before. He believed me, but we still had to go to Nicole's room. She was sitting on her bed holding a big teddy bear in her arms. I looked into her eyes before I asking her why she had lied. She couldn't answer. "Nicole, you know the truth, and I hope God will punish you," I said to her. I then gave her my salary but she looked down and refused to take it. When Dee heard this she was very angry and promised she would never speak to Nicole again. Two weeks later Nicole left her boyfriend and I noticed her with a boy who had come to drink there. At closing time they left together. The next morning I heard someone screaming.

When I got there I found security beating Nicole's new boyfriend. Nicole was standing next to two boxes full of porno movies. They told me the boy had been caught stealing from the sex shop. The boy had already been badly beaten but they carried on. I was frightened – it was the first time I had seen someone beating a white person. I thought a white person wouldn't survive a beating because white skin looks so fragile.

Suddenly Morocka arrived and I was relieved when he stopped them. Morocka wanted to know what had happened. He turned to me and asked what had happened. I said they were beating the boy when I arrived. I said I had seen him drinking in the sex shop. Morocka didn't think the boy had done anything wrong and he let him go though he fired Nicole. Dee and her boyfriend started smoking cocaine a few weeks later and it made me very sad.

She was a beautiful person and I could see the drug was killing her. I tried to tell her she was turning into something bad but she couldn't do anything to stop herself. Dee was wasting all her money on cocaine. Sometimes I lent her money I knew she wouldn't pay back. I didn't mind that I wouldn't get my money back because of everything she had done for me without expecting anything in return.

At the time my stomach was growing bigger and I was getting desperate. I started smoking more than forty cigarettes a day. I gave birth to a baby girl.

My health was bad, but I couldn't tell Morocka or anybody else because I was afraid I would be fired. I worked in constant pain. Dee was destroying herself with cocaine and there was no one I could talk to or share my pain with. A month later Dee left. I was the only one left in the bar. The sex shop was losing customers, and I was afraid I would lose my job. To stop this I served doubles. When the customer paid for a drink I would give them two. The problem was Raja was responsible for the stock, and soon he saw that all the alcohol was disappearing. He didn't wait for my explanation. He went straight to Morocka who called for me, and I found him seated behind his desk drinking a glass of whisky. He asked me whether I had eaten. When I said no he picked up the phone and ordered a couple of omelettes.

I couldn't tell if he was angry with me, but I knew I had to tell him the truth. "Innocent, are you stealing from me?" he asked. "No, Mr Morocka," I replied and explained why. At last he smiled and told me not to do anything without asking him.

I worked until about four in the afternoon when Boxer arrived and told me that Lieutenant-Colonel Moses Drago had been killed in an ambush. I walked slowly to the wall and leaned against it. I felt as though there was no point in being alive, but I had to be strong because of my son, Moses Drago Jr. I went downstairs and asked Raja if I could use the phone. I nearly collapsed when Drago himself answered the phone. That was the first call I had made since I had left Uganda.

When I told him that someone told me he was dead, he laughed and said he was stronger than ever. I was confused. Drago too had heard I was no longer alive. He was very happy to hear that I was alive and begged me to return. I told him no. He promised he would talk to the NRA and explain the whole thing. But I knew the NRA and going back would mean risking my life. Besides, I knew Drago could never give me what I really wanted, which was freedom. Before saying goodbye, Drago wanted me to promise I would look after his children some day. With a smile I said yes and told him I would call the next day. At around six o'clock I called and Eric, Drago's younger brother, answered.

Eric couldn't speak and I guessed something terrible had happened. I started crying still holding the phone in my hands, with a faint hope that I was wrong.

Then I heard numerous voices of people around Eric. My last hope had been taken away. Eric told me that Drago was dead. I called him again a day later, but I never found out how Drago died. Lieutenant-Colonel Moses Drago, Lieutenant-Colonel Bruce and Major Moses Kanabi: all gone within four years.

My childhood was gone and everyone I had loved was melting away. My mother and my sisters were gone and I was alone. I needed love desperately but I didn't know where to find it. I just wanted to put my head in someone's hands. I knew very well that no matter how much I cried I would never get any of this back. I forced myself to hate everyone who had died far away from me – the love I felt for them was killing me like a lethal injection. I tried to forget everything but it was impossible. I was often tempted to take drugs but every time I saw what drugs did to people I stopped myself. Instead I drank heavily and lost my job. It was then I realised I was losing the battle.

I decided to go for help to someone who used to come to the Chelsea to watch the strippers. I gave him a call and asked him if I could go and stay with him. I only stayed with him for a short time but soon he changed and got tired of feeding me because he got nothing in return.

I decided to run away from this man, and since I had nothing, I decided to take some of his things, wondering if he would be hurt. This kind of thing happened to me often. It really hurts to sleep with people just so you can survive. I had to do everything, good and bad, in order to survive because it was all I had – I had to earn money that way.

It hurt so much to let the last proof of my existence – my body, melt away.

Part Five

A Way Out

A Time to Be

FOUR YEARS WENT BY BEFORE I FINALLY found a way out. I desperately needed time to process what I had been through. I was alone. I had a letter in my hands I had to deliver to the United Nations High Commissioner for Refugees. I entered the huge building and the girl at reception didn't seem to listen to what I said, she just stared with her mouth wide open. I was an African dressed in white with a white scarf, just like a Muslim from Mecca.

I handed her the letter, and when I saw her take it, I cried. She made a call, spoke briefly and a minute later I followed a lady into her office. Her name was Pamela, and I sat down without introducing myself. I was asked to tell her everything that had happened to me. The way she asked me was the key I had lost. In a split second everything appeared before my eyes. I couldn't speak. This woman who seemed to care so much freed me. I crouched down deep in the chair, so deep that everything turned black. She couldn't handle my reaction and told me she would be back.

Pamela returned with a man who took my hand and led me to his office. He asked me if I smoked, gave me a cigarette and told me to let it all out. Then he quietly looked into his desk while I cried like a child. When I had stopped crying, the man introduced himself as Burt Leenschool. He wanted to know how I'd got this letter. I told him what had happened.

Some months before I had met a Ugandan man who told me he lived in England, travelling all over the world to promote his organisation which was fighting against Museveni's government. When the man mentioned Museveni, I remembered Drago, my friends and myself. I joined his group.

In the South African group he had fifteen members, many of whom were ex-Museveni soldiers. The group leader was a Muslim. He told us we weren't the only ones who had been treated so badly. I was so desperate to join the struggle that all suspicion was forgotten. Once again I would be able to do what I was good at. This time it would be of my own free will, and I knew very well what I would be fighting for. Later the leader rented an office in the middle of Johannesburg. At the meetings we would watch movies to commemorate Idi Amin's words.

At my fifth meeting I heard the comrades talk about Major Kasaija, who was in the Ugandan army. Kasaija was a very good friend of mine, and I wanted to know more about where he was at that time. When I heard he had been brought to work at the Ugandan Embassy in South Africa, I couldn't wait to see him. I thought he would understand me and I wanted him to tell me what to do to get back home. I started looking for the Embassy's telephone number.

I spoke to Kasaija, but he couldn't remember me. I was sure it was he because of the language he spoke. To refresh his memory I told him about my whole history in the army. He invited me over to his office. Though I knew him well, I still didn't want to risk my life so I went with a Zambian man. I told him to wait at reception. "If you hear me scream, please run for help," I said. When I entered the office, it was a man I had never seen before. He stood up and greeted me with respect. Probably because of what he knew about me.

The moment I saw him I could tell he had never been a soldier. He claimed to know the real Major Kasaija. He offered me tea, but I refused anything unless it had been sealed. It was after closing time, and I was alone with him and his secretary. I felt safer, but my eyes still couldn't stay in one place. The man said he believed I was the victim of a big mistake. He was convinced I was a hero who deserved better. Now I believed he was on my side, so I decided to tell him about my involvement in the meetings. I tried to explain what happened to all of us who were betrayed. Suddenly he changed. I was impressed to see what he had been hiding. Now he seemed prepared to go to war.

He demanded that I deliver my comrades in return for immunity. I could only laugh inside at this man who believed me wrong. And anyway, I didn't believe what he said about immunity. He gave me some money and I promised to return soon after my research was done. I knew I had convinced him and that he didn't know that I had got money for nothing. Weeks later I went to a party organised by Uganda Airlines.

At around eleven o'clock, some guys promised to drive me back to Johannesburg. I was drunk and I'm not sure what I said about

Museveni's government – though I'm sure I used stories from my past to earn their respect. We left at around midnight. I couldn't tell whether or not we were going in the right direction because I didn't know Pretoria that well. Suddenly we stopped at a building and two of them dragged me to an apartment. I was ordered to strip myself naked. They searched my clothes and when they asked for my passport I told them it was at home. I was asked if I was in contact with Kashilingi and I said no.

By early morning I had sobered up. Two of them gripped me firmly while the other stabbed me in my backside with something like an ice pick. They knew who I was and they wanted to know what I had said and to whom. I told them my side of the story and why I had run away, but they still called me a deserter.

They assured me this was nothing compared to what would happen if I were taken back to Uganda. After they had taken away my last sense of dignity, I told them to take me back to Uganda to face whatever they had decided to do to me. But they could not move me because I was very weak and sick. I saved myself by making myself sicker.

Every time they said that it was time to go I would make myself sicker. This trick saved my life, but eventually the time came when they wanted to take me back to Uganda. We got in the car and drove into town. We stopped at a traffic light in busy Pretoria.

Just when the driver reached for the gears I distracted them by punching the rear window. By the time they saw what had happened I had opened the door and leapt out.

Saviours

I WENT STRAIGHT TO THE HOSPITAL. My wounds healed eventually but my spirit had been broken. I had been under their rule of terror for six months and it still feels like it was years. I couldn't have been much more than a ghost when I got to the hospital reception. After an operation I went to Home Affairs where Tinus Van Jaarsveld received me. "Rebel! What happened to you? You look like a ghost!" He was truly shocked when he saw the marks. I gave him the letter from the hospital and managed to tell him what happened.

He took me straight to another office where he repeated my words to the woman there. Heidi listened carefully as I told her about my life and how I became a child soldier. It was hard to talk and I realised for' the first time I wasn't in control anymore. Since I became a child soldier no woman had ever seen me cry, and there I was, crying in front of a woman. I also hated crying in front of a civilian because I thought they were too stupid to understand things. Still, I had no choice because there were only civilians in control.

When I had finished my story she seemed to forget about me. She looked down angrily and began typing a letter. She put it in an envelope and addressed it to the United Nations High Commissioner for Refugees.

That was how I ended up at the UN with Burt Leenschool. After telling him my story I looked down, and there was silence for a while. Then Burt told me he wanted someone to check my wounds. He called a woman, Victoria Stofile, who checked me. The next day I was sent to the trauma clinic in Johannesburg. The woman there, Francis Spencer, was very kind, but her questions made me feel completely mad. Maybe I was crazy at the time. I felt a voice inside me begging me to ask for help – at the same time I really had to stop myself from jumping around, screaming and shouting in front of her. I was so afraid to remember because I was terrified – what would happen if they suddenly rejected me?

I came to love her because she listened to me for hours. I was still in control. I tried not to let anything I said affect my soul. I knew I was a fighter because I had managed all along. Now I was in someone else's hands and I didn't know in which direction they would throw me. The woman didn't give up. She tried to convince me that not everyone wanted to harm me. Little by little I began to trust her.

I was overwhelmed with so many intense emotions I had to let out only a little at a time. I had become the gatekeeper to my consciousness, but the pressure was so high that I had to give in. I lost control of myself and everything went around and around in my mind at once, twenty-four hours a day. I was terrified when I knew I had to go back for another consultation. I felt like shouting "No!" only I feared her reaction and I didn't want her to be upset with me. In my past I had only learned to say yes – even to the most terrible things. The trauma clinic found me a psychiatrist, Barend Foster, and I was seeing both of them.

The UN had put me in a hotel room and every time I had to go the psychiatrist, a Land Cruiser with UN flags picked me up. The psychiatrist was Afrikaans and in his late forties. He was a tall, strong-looking man with a beard. I was put on medication that replaced my nightmares with far-out dreams. I could laugh in my dreams instead of crying in them. The psychiatrist seemed to be helping me in many ways. I started accepting who I was, and learned that the bad things I did were not my fault. I also started opening up a bit to other people.

It was ten in the morning, and I was standing in front of the hotel when a car arrived. The driver said he was taking me to Burt. I was standing in front of his desk when Burt asked me which country I wanted to be resettled in. I thought I hadn't heard correctly and I asked him what he had meant. He repeated himself, saying, "I want you to tell me in which country you would like to live."

"The United States of America," I replied.

"Do you know anybody there?" he asked and I said no. He told me he didn't think it was a good idea, but he was sending my statement to Geneva and he was sure they would decide what was best for me.

I couldn't believe my ears. All I could feel was a tingling sensation all over my body. My chair was getting hot and I stood up, excited, and screamed. Not because I was going to another country but because I had been given the right to make a choice. I felt so much excitement I didn't know what to do with it. If I hadn't been afraid of Burt I would have hugged him so hard some of his bones would have snapped. We still had to talk about my son. I hadn't spoken to Moses Drago Jr since his father's death.

I didn't know where to begin. I had the phone number of a friend of mine and Burt allowed me to call. My friend told me that before Drago died he decided to leave my son with Rita, his girlfriend. Rita didn't want to let him go. I think she loved him because he had stayed with her since I took him from my sister Margie, though at that moment I didn't care about how Rita felt. I only wanted my son.

When the UN offices in Uganda finally managed to contact Rita, she told Drago's family. They didn't trust her and accused her of trying to steal my son and they decided to take care of him. Rita had never been an easy person, and she wasn't prepared to give in without a fight, but she lost the case because she was not related to Drago or me. Burt told me he was doing all he could to reunite me with my son. Everything seemed to go in the right direction and all I could do was to wait for Geneva to decide my fate. The love and care I received from the people at the UN offices made me feel like a child.

The smile I thought I'd lost forever was beginning to come back, and I was learning to trust people again.

The medication I was given by the psychiatrist made me restless, and I felt an urge to tell everyone about my past. I still felt ashamed to let the real China out because I thought people would laugh or run away. Since I desperately wanted to talk I decided to tell a different story. I told everyone I was a Canadian on holiday and when they asked what I was doing, I would say I was a student. At home most people lied about who they were and what had happened to them. It didn't matter that they had no food – they would still smile and say, "I'm okay." Most people prefer not to talk about their struggles because no one wants to be ashamed.

Far Away from Africa

"GUESS WHAT? YOU CAN GO AND LIVE IN DENMARK!" When he mentioned Denmark I became sad, and when he asked why, I said, "Mr Burt, I do not want to go to Denmark because it's near Africa".

"Oh, no – I'm sorry. I should have told you right away! Denmark is very far away from Africa." When he said it was on the border with Germany, all my fear was gone. I sat down in the waiting room and asked myself what kind of a country is Denmark to decide to accept me, China, with a broken life and no education. How could they have felt my pain, even though they are so far away?

I walked back to my hotel where I sat and tried to imagine what Denmark might be like.

Two days later I was taken to the Danish Embassy where I was given a travel document. Back at the hotel I met a German man named Alex Kugler. Kugler was part of a group of German medical students who had come to work at a South African hospital. Kugler was a Christian and spoke a little Swahili. He had learned it on a tour in Kenya and Tanżania. He told me that after finishing his studies he would like to live in Africa to help the children there. I admired him and soon I told him he should let me know when he was going to church. In the evening Kugler came into my room and told me someone was waiting to drive us to the church. Outside a BMW was waiting, and when we got into the car a man introduced himself as Willy van Wyk.

When I realised he was Afrikaans I became afraid, but I decided to take a chance. On our way Willy told me about Jesus and how much he had improved his life, and because Willy drove an expensive BMW, I believed his testimony – though I did believe that God had the last word. It was a huge church where black and white all sat together. I sat next to Kugler and on the other side of me sat an old Afrikaans couple.

I wasn't used to sitting in one place for long and I was getting bored, but I managed to stay put until the service was over. Before returning to the hotel Kugler had a cup of coffee and I had a piece of cake.

The next evening, Van Wyk came to fetch us again. This time he took us to his friend's house. It was a very cold winter's evening. The house was so warm we didn't need to wear our jackets. I was the only black person, and when a Chinese girl walked in I was relieved. The prayers started with a song and afterwards we were told to take off our shoes and socks. I was embarrassed because my socks were full of holes. I tried to take them off as carefully as I could, and I managed to do it without anyone noticing.

An Afrikaans lady had the water ready. She told us she was going to wash our feet just like Jesus did with his disciples. I nearly asked for a cigarette – I felt like running away. After they washed our feet we were told to pray in silence. I felt unable to pray.

Was this love or was it a coincidence I had come to church on a ceremonial day when they washed their feet? I saw no hatred there, and none of the remaining apartheid that lurked around the corner. These people seemed to have grown up in an entirely different South Africa, but I just wasn't sure. Back at the hotel Kugler told me he and some friends would be going to camp in the mountains, but he assured me he would be back before I went to Denmark.

I also met Judith Osseforth, a German girl who was in the same group as Kugler. She was in her last year of medical studies. Later on she introduced me to Alexander Müller and Eberhard Reithmeier. I had a good time with them. On the day before my departure they took me to a restaurant where I had a great meal. When we'd finished our meal we ate ice cream before we returned to the hotel. I couldn't fall asleep – I sat on my bed thinking about Denmark. Although I had had a very difficult time in South Africa, I still felt pain about leaving it

The next day I felt sad and excited. I couldn't think or be in one place. It was very cold but I was feeling hot. At one point I thought I was having a heart attack.

I was standing at the reception when Kugler arrived. He hurried to his room and after having dropped his luggage he came to see me and we walked to the famous South African Union Buildings. We walked all over the place taking photos but I don't remember what I saw because my mind was not with me.

At six o'clock in the evening, Pamela arrived in a UN car and took me to the airport. She made sure everything was ready and when she said goodbye I cried because she reminded me of my sister Margie who I hadn't seen or talked to for four years.

I walked through the hallway until I came to a huge place filled with chairs. Some of the people were already seated. I didn't understand where I was, whether it was a plane or a theatre, so I asked one of the girls standing there. "Is this a house or a plane?" All of them started laughing and I joined in.

They showed me my seat and soon two Spanish people sat down next to me. When the plane was about to take off I saw that everybody had a small table in front of them, only I couldn't find mine.

When they said we must put on our belts, I struggled but someone helped me with everything. Early the next morning, we arrived at Frankfurt airport, and there I boarded another plane. I arrived in Copenhagen at twelve o'clock on 21 June 1999.

I got off the plane and a tall man called my name. He greeted me and took me by the hand. We went straight to the police office. They cleared me and then he handed me over to a woman who introduced herself as Birgitte Knudsen. Her colleague Karl Erik was with her. The three of us drove to their office where I was introduced to Pia. I had never been cared for like that before. It was then I knew that some day I would come to love Denmark. Later that day Birgitte and Karl showed me around Copenhagen. After the tour they took me to a place called Diakonisse Stiftelsen.

I was given a room. Everything was new to me. I had my lunch in a huge dining room at a large table. It felt so luxurious I felt as if I didn't belong there.

I found it a little easier to adopt the ways of the Danes because I had been a stranger before. Two days later while I was having breakfast, a man in his late fifties started making his coffee. After having finished he offered me a cup. Though I didn't drink coffee, I didn't say no – I didn't want to offend him. The coffee was very strong, so I closed my eyes and drank it. He introduced himself as Knud Held Hansen. Hansen was married and had three grown children, Jette and twin boys named Carsten and Jens. Hansen lived in Aalborg, and he was in Copenhagen on business. He made me feel relaxed. I didn't feel so defensive anymore. I noticed him looking at my head, as though he thought something was missing. Just before we finished our coffee, he asked: "Where is your hair? When is it coming back? I think you would look pretty with hair."

I found it easy to talk to him – I felt as if I'd known him for years. He asked me if I wanted to see Copenhagen. The first thing he took me to see was The Little Mermaid and on our way back he asked me if I wanted to see Bakken. As with everything else, I didn't know what he was talking about but I didn't want to part yet so I agreed immediately. We parked the car and walked onto a broad dirt road that led through a forest with big old trees. All around us were happy people walking around or being driven in horse carriages.

I was enchanted by the coachmen in strange uniforms driving the horses that walked as if they were in a pleasant dream.

In the clearing of the wood, huge fires burned and Hansen told me they were burning witches. I stood and looked at one of the bonfires but saw no witches. I was even more mystified. Finally we entered an amusement park. The place was overcrowded with people busy amusing themselves.

Then I saw the huge machines swinging people into the air and down again. All of them were laughing and shouting. It was heaven – I couldn't wait to join in. Hansen stood and watched me swing like a child. I was wild with every game there and he thought it was very funny. When I had had enough I was really hungry so we went to an Italian restaurant. As we sat waiting for our pizzas a couple greeted us. They talked very differently from Hansen and the people at Diakonisse Stiftelsen, and I was right when I told Hansen they weren't Danish. They were Swedish but Hansen still understood everything they said.

In the evening, back at Diakonisse Stiftelsen, Hansen had his strong coffee while I enjoyed a cup of tea. As we sat there his cell phone rang and I spoke to his wife and daughter. The next day Hansen returned to Aalborg and I was left in tears, though I knew I would see him again. He treated me like one of his children and from that day on I saw him as my real father. The love Hansen showed me during that time made me think that there had been a good reason for the USA saying no to me.

In Denmark life is treated so carefully that even an animal has rights. I was no longer told what to do or whom to hate and kill. The most beautiful thing was I no longer had to live my life for others, and no force ever makes me act against my will.

But even with all this freedom I still have the fear I carried as a soldier.

My féar seems to be permanent and it feels like a mark for life. In my sleep I still see the shadows of my fellow child soldiers and friends who took their own lives in order to escape. Most of my pain is over now, but the war is still on and there are many children whom, I believe, are still crying for our help.

The battle is not over, so lift up your voice and demand the glory.

Epilogue

SINCE MOVING TO DENMARK, China has been studying Danish. Recently she began working in a kindergarten with children between three and six years of age. The Danish government makes sure she has enough money to live on. China is currently trying to get custody of her son who is still in Uganda. Once she has accomplished this, she will start the search for her daughter in South Africa. Visit China's website at www.xchildsoldier.org

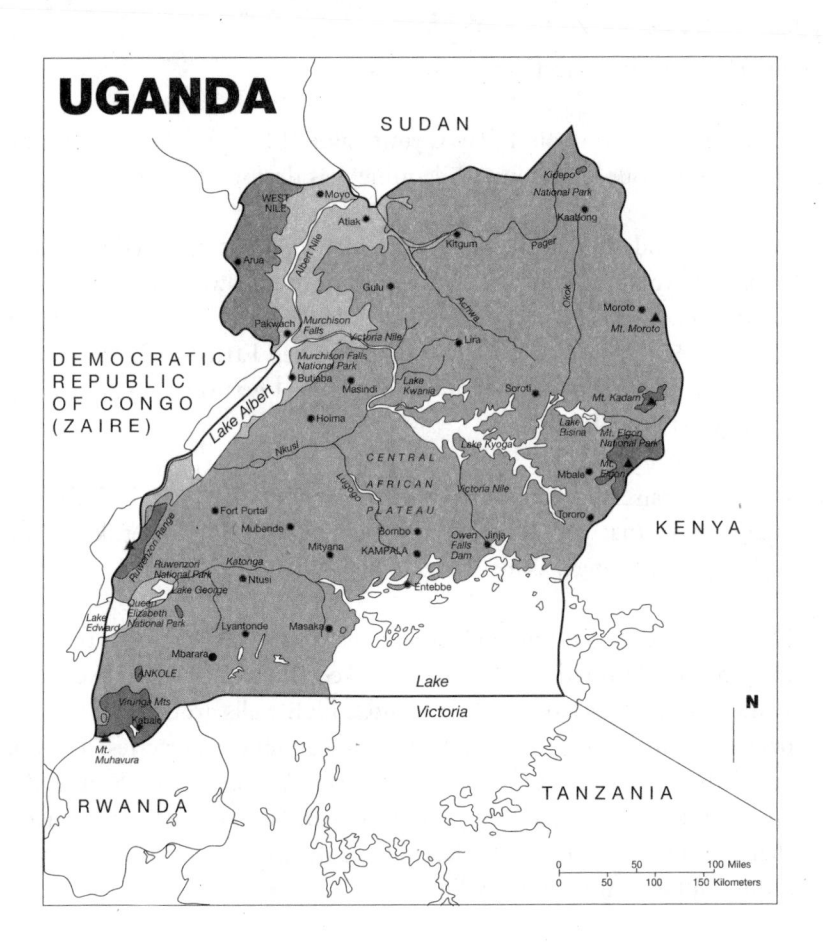

UGANDA

Dr Milton Obote became president of Uganda in 1962 when it became an independent state. In 1971, Idi Amin toppled Obote in a military coup. In 1980, Obote became the Ugandan president for a second time.

In January 1986, Yoweri Museveni and the NRA ousted Milton Obote. Museveni has been president of Uganda ever since.

To Yoweri Museveni

I shed my blood for you. I played your game although I didn't know the rules. I saw your face shine while mine was drained of its colour.

While my body did all the dirty work for you, my soul asked me questions only you could answer. But you wouldn't answer – you were hiding in a place where we weren't allowed. You were afraid of my soul and told your bodyguards not to let it in, and when I tried to force my way in you ordered them to catch me and steal it. I was running away from those guns like a fugitive.

I tried to raise my voice for you to hear, but the hunt had already begun. Now that you got what you wanted, you don't even know my name. It's so strange. Why don't we play anymore?

Didn't I raise my weapon high enough for you? Maybe it's just that you got what you wanted. Why didn't you keep your promises? I've spent years trying to work out why. Is it those high walls around your house or is it the men with the guns that make you ignore our cries? Do you remember us? You promised us new lives. We were with you at the enemy lines and so many of us were killed, and yet you say it wasn't that bad. I wish I had known that putting my life in your hands was like falling in love with a hungry lion.

Your child soldier

China Keitetsi